Greetings to
Chris
from the author,
Camille F. Jones
5-15-...

Thank Heaven for Laughter

The Life and Times of a Rio Grande Valley Girl

by
Camille Johnston Jones

authorHOUSE™

1663 LIBERTY DRIVE, SUITE 200
BLOOMINGTON, INDIANA 47403
(800) 839-8640
WWW.AUTHORHOUSE.COM

© 2006 Camille Johnston Jones. All Rights Reserved.

No part of this book may be reproduced, stored in a retrieval system, or transmitted by any means without the written permission of the author.

First published by AuthorHouse 01/11/06

ISBN: 1-4259-9988-3 (sc)
ISBN: 1-4208-7999-5 (dj)

Library of Congress Control Number: 2005907787

Printed in the United States of America
Bloomington, Indiana

This book is printed on acid-free paper.

To my family I offer my thanks for their help in remembering details and incidents which have been included in this effort. I want to also express my appreciation to the girls in the office who helped organize my work and to the Parlor Sunday School Class for encouraging me to put my stories in print.

Contents

Foreword ix

Part One - The Early Years

The Family Heritage 3
Mercedes - A Generation Ago 11
The Year at Hockaday 13
Europe with the YMCA Tour 17
The Farm Bureau Contest 23
The Rio Hondo Bridge - 1958 26
Hawaii 28
College Friends and Events 32
Our Wedding and Honeymoon 35
The Wedding in Baton Rouge 38
The Dallas Wedding 40

Part Two - Special Events

Moving to Donna 45
Hunting in Texas 49
Trout Fishing in the Channel 71
Bass Fishing in Mexico 74
Parasailing at Padre - 1984 77
Rafting on the River 80
Snowmobiling - 1993 83
Hot Air Ballooning 85
Tee-Heeing in Tennessee 88

Part Three - Travels with Family and Friends

Real de Catorce - 1970	93
The Great Southwest - 1971	95
France For a Few Francs - 1972	99
England on a Shoestring	104
On the Road Again, to Guadalajara!	108
Mazatlan - 1976	110
Cancun - 1978	114
Easter in Cancun	116
Britain, Here We Come!	118
Here Come the British!	125
The Jungles of Campeche - 1979	127
San Miguel Allende via Real de Catorce	130
San Miguel de Allende Revisited	133
New York City with the Girls - 2002	135
North Zulch, Texas - 2005	140
Dinner at Dripping Springs - 2005	143
Corpus Christi - 2005	145
Epilogue - Parting Words	147

Foreword

As I begin this endeavor, I stop to thank God for the many blessings He has bestowed on me throughout my lifetime. He has always been there to guide, support, and protect me, even when I found myself way, way out on a limb or put myself in a precarious position. I pray He will be honored by the words I choose and the message I hope to convey to the readers of this book: laughter is good for the soul as well as the body. Laughter is a gift from God bestowed on humans alone (except for hyenas, of course). It lifts your spirits as nothing else can do; it puts a smile on your face and joy in your heart. It lightens the load you bear, even in the most difficult of situations.

My life has been filled with many humorous experiences and I hope you will find them entertaining. I have included memories from my youth, special events after our marriage and the birth of our children, and some traveling experiences with close friends across the years. Some of the episodes included in this book were amusing at the time and led to laughter right away; others took several years of re-telling and pondering before the real humor in them could be fully appreciated.

I hope you will sit back, relax and enjoy!

Part One - The Early Years

The Family Heritage

I was the last of five children born to Robert Hartman and Anne Vanderslice Johnston. My father was a medical doctor who had been stationed in New Orleans, Louisiana, during part of World War II and he was on staff at a new army hospital located on Canal Street. When my mother was rushed to the hospital for delivery, her regular physician could not be located and my dad had do the honors. Normally, a doctor doesn't choose to attend to the medical needs of his immediate family, but, in this instance, we all were happy to have him there!

My parents were Christian missionaries in China from 1930 until 1935 and married there on January 1, 1931. The wedding was quite an event. Mother was carried to the service in a traditional wedding rickshaw by several young Chinese men and the ceremony was performed by a fellow missionary, Dwight Kirkland West.

It was two years later that they had their first child, Robert, Jr., who only survived a few days due to respiratory complications. My parents were anxious to have another child right away but that didn't happen. After their return to the United States several years later, they decided to adopt a child and made applications to several agencies. Little did my parents know what surprises Mother Nature had in store for them: Eloise (August,1937), Walter (April,1939), Bobby (April,1940) and Yours Truly (August,1941). Mother was pregnant for the better part of four consecutive years! You can imagine all the difficulties of raising four children just a year apart - she had to have help or lose her sanity. And to add to her problems, my father was often away long hours tending to his patients. Sometimes I think he stayed away longer than necessary, just to avoid some of the headaches (and noise) four little children can cause. Each of our parents had interesting lives themselves, and I want to introduce them to you at the outset of this endeavor.

Robert Hartman Johnston

I can't find the family history on my father's side of the family but it was etched into our memories long ago. My father was the youngest of seven siblings. His father was Professor Walter Ewing Johnston, President of Bethel College in Tennessee, and his mother was Betty May Johnston. The family lived in Enid, Mississippi, during most of my father's childhood years and he left home to further his education when he was fourteen. He attended a small Presbyterian school in Maryville, Tennessee, and then moved on to the University of Florida for his undergraduate degree. He received his medical degree at Vanderbilt University in 1927 and did his internship at Fitzsimmons in Colorado. At the early age of 25, he headed to China as a medical missionary. Wow!

My father was fortunate to be part of a very well-educated family. He grew up not only with textbook knowledge but also with an appreciation of the fine arts. He learned to play the violin and the piano at a very early age, and they were a source of pleasure for him and his acquaintances his entire life. Sitting down at the piano and playing before his family or an audience of 500 was great fun for him. He could play Bach or he could play Broadway, depending on his mood at the time. He had an ear for music; it was easy for him to accompany others without the music in front of him and so he was called upon to play in numerous situations. Graduation exercises were always on his list of musical performances, as well as the annual Rio Grande Valley ten-piano classical concerts. My parents often played duets at church. Father would play the piano and Mother would play the organ. Their duets were always a meaningful part of the worship service.

Thank Heaven *for* Laughter

Robert Hartman was an out-going, gregarious person. He loved to laugh. He loved a good joke (nothing risque), but anything funny. Father often kidded around with the office personnel, his close friends, his children and his wife. (Mother didn't always appreciate his humor but everyone else did.) He loved to tease others and often came downstairs during a bridge party wearing a funny mask or outrageous clothes. He liked practical jokes (which didn't really hurt anyone), like the plastic ice cube with a bug in it or the hand-shake gag where you shock the person holding out his hand toward you or the can of candy where the insides spring out at you. Father loved life and he loved people. It was obvious in his daily routine at home and in the workplace as well. (I can still hear his laughter after forty years.)

One of my parents' favorite pastimes was playing bridge. Father liked to play aggressively and often bid a slam just to prove a point. Nothing made him happier than to win a trick with a deuce. (His smile always turned into a very broad grin.) He was lucky at cards but he was also fairly knowledgeable of the game. No need to rehash the playing of the hand - his face said it all. Mother was a bit more demure in her card playing. She never tried to take the limelight or outdo her husband at the bridge table, but her skill was well-noted by other members of their bridge club.

Medicine was Father's chosen field and he often told us how fortunate he felt to have been called to that field. He loved his work and told us time and again how much his patients meant to him. Never was he more excited than the night he came in to dinner announcing he had just delivered healthy triplets. Never was he so sad as when he had to report the death of one of his patients. It really made a difference to him. He often asked Mother to drive him on his afternoon calls and they would return late in the evening. Sometimes it would be a delivery or a patient too ill to come to the clinic but often it would be a routine visit. He enjoyed being needed and he enjoyed having "Mrs. J." at his side.

Father built a clinic behind our house not only for the comfort and convenience of his patients, but for himself as well. He had a nurse on staff 24 hours a day and could be called in at the last minute to deliver a baby or perform minor surgery on a patient. Sometimes he was called to the clinic in the wee hours of the morning and delivered babies in his slacks and a pajama shirt! (The mothers never complained.)

During the 50's the bracero (Mexican temporary worker) program was in effect for several years and Father's clinic was filled to capacity for most of the summer. He very often saw as many as 50 patients on Sundays and often had to hire additional nurses to cope with the number of patients he saw. He felt their plight and wanted to give them the best medical care possible but had little time left over for himself or his family.

Traveling was another one of Father's favorite pastimes. He didn't believe in giving his children an abundance of material things, but he did believe in giving them a really good education. In his mind, that included traveling to the places you read about in books and meeting the people who lived there on a first-name basis. He thought walking in another person's shoes would provide great insights into a particular culture. Grouping people into specific categories left out the individuals who, for the most part, were just like us in their wants and ambitions. Eloise went to Europe for six weeks when she was 16, Bob and I went when we were 16 and 14 respectively, and when Walt was 20, Father took him to Russia. What an education those experiences were for us!

Going to church was mandatory in our household. No excuse, medical or otherwise, was tolerated for not being present. If you wanted to go out of the house (perhaps to an afternoon movie), you had to have been in church earlier in the day. We only lived a block away from the small Presbyterian church in Mercedes and we were there every Sunday I can remember. The congregation was small and that made it all the more important for everyone to attend. We became an extended family to one another and when a member was lost to death or re-location, it was felt by all.

Father was very much involved in school and community activities and often gave talks on a variety of health and hygiene issues. He often invited the young men in these groups over to our house for a swim after meetings, and if they didn't have the necessary bathing attire, he simply turned off the lights and let them swim in the raw.

My father was quite the disciplinarian and he demanded respect. We didn't call him, "Daddy" or "Pop". We called him "Father". It wasn't until I was eighteen, and far off in Hawaii, that he wrote me a note on several of his prescription pads and signed it, "Love, Hartman." Actually he drew a heart and added the "man" to that. I cried when I read the letter. It was the most endearing gesture he ever made toward me. Oh, he had always told me that he loved me, but this was extra special. He didn't sign it "Daddy", but that's what he meant.

During World War II, Father served overseas and was gone for nearly four years. He had many interesting stories to tell, but particularly enjoyed telling the one about the bomb that landed in his tent just minutes after he had left the camp. He also like to tell about his trip to Manchuria with Kirk West when they were missionaries in China. The people in that part of the world had never seen anyone with his coloring (sandy-blond hair and bright blue eyes). They thought he must have been some kind of a god. Father enjoyed it immensely.

His grandchildren were extra special to him. It was too bad he only got to spend time with the first four of the fifteen his children were eventually going to have. However, he managed to dote on the ones he did know and was pleased to learn that more were on the way when he became ill in 1964.

When he was diagnosed with cancer of the pancreas at the age of 57, he accepted the fact and made the best of the last few months he had to live. He asked that we not weep for him; he had enjoyed a marvelous life, had seen his children educated and happily married, and he was ready for whatever the good Lord had in store for him. He expected to see his deceased family members in heaven and set a model of "hope for a better tomorrow" for those of us left behind. Donating his body parts to science was his last wish.

Dr. Robert Hartman Johnston was no god; he was simply a good Christian doctor who wanted to leave this world a better place when he died. We think he did that. He also left us the memory of his roaring laughter.

Anne Ellen Vanderslice Johnston West

Our mother was quite a different personality. She never sought attention and while she enjoyed listening to Father's jokes and stories, she seldom laughed out loud. It wasn't ladylike in her estimation and she had been taught to be a proper lady. (She tried to teach me to be a proper lady also, but things just didn't turn out as well as she hoped.)

We had a great rapport: she was the mother and I was the baby of the family. She doted on me extensively and I loved every minute of it. She doted on my siblings as well, but I WAS THE BABY and seemed to get more than my share of the attention. She was almost 36 when she had me and she was almost 96 when she died in May of 2001; we had a long, wonderful relationship.

Mother had an adventuresome life and wrote a manuscript about it for the family when she was in her 70's. It would take pages and pages to give you the details, but let me just say that she was born in Buchanan, Michigan, in 1905 to Dwight Leslie and Annie Ellen Vanderslice; she graduated from and then taught at Maryville College in Tennessee; she was captain of the college girls' basketball team her senior year (bloomer uniforms); she climbed Mt. Fuji in Japan during her 20's, and then went on to China to serve as a missionary for five years.

After my parents returned to the States, Mother had four children, one right after the other, and then she spent the next 60 years of her life looking after them. She was always there to help with the older grandchildren when new ones arrived and often traveled thousands of miles to be there.

Mother supported us in all our school activities. She was President of the P.T.A., she baked pies and brownies for school functions, she held an office in the Band Booster Club, and she even chaperoned our senior trip to Bandera.

As wonderful a mother as she was to us, a better wife she was to Father. She was his private secretary and kept all his financial records straight. She entertained unexpected guests at the last minute with charm and graciousness. Many social activities and functions had to be attended alone, as he was often called away to see a patient. She spent nearly every afternoon in the kitchen and dinner was on the table every evening at six for the six of us. (Everyone had to be present or give a good reason why we couldn't be there.) Although she often differed from Father in her opinions as how to handle difficulties, she never voiced them in front of the children. His decision in family matters was always final.

She never lost her love of travel. Very often, at the drop of a hat, she packed all of us in the car and drove off to Mississippi to visit relatives or to New York City to see some plays and visit other family members. She kept in touch with the whole family by mail and planned her trips so as to include visits with old college friends as well as cousins, nieces, and nephews. Perhaps her most famous trip was the time she arranged her schedule to take my sister to New York City for her sailing to Europe via Seattle. (Mother's niece was getting married there and she wanted to see all her Vanderslice relatives.) I think we put 6,000 miles on the odometer that trip.

After my father died, Mother devoted most of her time to church work. She became Moderator of the Women of the Church for the Mission Presbytery and it kept her busy for a number of years. She continued to travel with other widows involved in church work and toured many mission sites in Africa and Korea.

Kirk West came back into Mother's life when she was 72 and he was 75. Mother went to visit a cousin in Medford, Oregon, and Kirk, now a widower, was preaching at the Presbyterian church there. He recognized her in the congregation and introduced her to the audience. Mother was smitten and in seven months' time, they were married in front of the fireplace at our house in Donna. They had eight wonderful years together before he died of cancer and she moved back to Mercedes.

It wasn't until she moved into our home about ten years ago that the mother/daughter roles reversed. She began to depend on me for decisions and support, instead of the other way around. One day she asked if I thought it would be okay if she declined giving the lesson at the church circle meetings. At the age of 92, I thought she had probably done her part.

Sometimes when I look in the mirror these days, I see her looking back at me. Many of the gestures she used, I am using. Some of the advice she offered to me (when asked), I am offering to others (when asked). My hands have age spots just like hers did. I have even learned to like cold cereal. I don't remember her laugh but I do remember her kind and gentle smile.

Grandmother Johnston, Mother and four children.

Mercedes - A Generation Ago

Our family moved to Mercedes, Texas, in 1946. Dr. Marion Lawler and my father had been classmates at Vanderbilt Medical School in Nashville during the mid 1920's and he was looking for a partner in his medical practice. What a great opportunity! What a great move! What a great place to raise a family! What a great place to make friends and create great memories!

Mercedes was a thriving, bustling town of about 12,000 people in the 1940's and 1950's. There were several banks, three movie theaters, a couple of pharmacies, several dress shops, and at least four or five restaurants on Texas Avenue. It boasted of having twenty-eight churches in the community and its own baseball team. Everyone knew everybody, or at least knew someone who knew someone who knew everybody. Precious little went on that wasn't seen or heard by someone who knew you or your family; that was good when you wanted a donation for a school project, but bad when you wanted to keep specific things private.

A great many of the friends I have today (Ann Farris, Margie Brooke, Elizabeth Dalton, Joan Reed, Pat Werner, Joanna Burgess, Charlene Childress, Buster Brown, Jimmy Duncan) are people who started school with me years and years ago. Time cannot erase the memories you create during your elementary and high school years and that is probably why class reunions are so popular. Classmates don't always agree on the details, but most remember that certain events did actually happen and they enjoy retelling them with their own slant. The girls usually talk about slumber parties, old boyfriends, hairstyles, and clothes. The boys usually talk about football games, recounting play after play after play after play.

One friend, in particular, Margie Collier, was an integral part of my happy childhood memories. Her family had the first swimming pool in town (filled with water from the canal, frogs and all), and all the kids loved to spend time at her house. We often played in her backyard and on one occasion, she and I decided to see how high we could swing in the hammock. We also thought it might be fun to see if Buttons, her Dalmatian, would enjoy swinging with us. Big mistake! After only a few minutes, Buttons threw up all over the two of us. We couldn't get him or ourselves out of the hammock fast enough. Guess we learned a lesson the hard way - it would be one of many more to come.

Another good friend of mine, Donnie Vollmer, was always getting into trouble at home. Her mother was quite a disciplinarian, and Donnie seemed to get caught every time she disobeyed her parents. She was always being grounded for one reason or another. Her parents both smoked and she liked to collect the cigarette butts, and, when her parents went out for the evening, she enjoyed putting them in a long cigarette holder and lighting them. I am sure she didn't inhale the smoke, but it was fun to pretend. (All the movie stars smoked in those days and she was just emulating them.)

One afternoon she called me in a panic, saying that she needed my help "on the double." When I got to her house, she said she had been painting her fingernails in the living room and had spilled nail polish on her mother's new rug. Boy, was she in trouble! She had tried using nail polish remover, but it had only made matters worse and her mom was due home any minute. We had to think fast! I suggested we move the furniture and turn the rug over to the other side so the stain couldn't been seen. What could we do about the strong smell of the polish remover? She decided that maybe a little smoke would help cover it and ran to get her stash of cigarette butts. When her mother arrived shortly afterwards, she told us she was very, very disappointed in us for smoking and that it would be best if we didn't spend time together for a while. Donnie was grounded again for a week or so, but was terribly happy that her mother never found out about the stain on the other side of the rug.

The Year at Hockaday

My sophomore year in high school (1956-1957) I attended The Hockaday School in Dallas, Texas, where my parents hoped I would receive a good education and learn some of the finer social skills.

The school was located on Greenville Avenue then and had both day students and boarders. The day I arrived on the premises, I was pleased to meet my roommate but was horrified to find that our room had bars across the windows. Those bars supported an outside canopy, making the room look prison-like.

We spent the first few weeks getting used to new rules, regulations, and schedules. There were very few free minutes! Breakfast was at 7:00 a.m.; followed by Chapel at 8:00 a.m.; followed by morning classes; followed by lunch; followed by afternoon classes; followed by sports activities, such as swimming or hockey and/or glee club; followed by dinner at 6:00 p.m.; followed by study hall at 7:00p.m.; and followed, finally, by "lights out" at 9:00 p.m. Each hall had a residence counselor who carefully watched over us and made sure we followed the rules.

There were girls from every part of the United States, as well as some from Mexico, Canada, and Europe attending school at Hockaday. I had a marvelous time getting to know a great many of them.

My roommate was from Fredericksburg, and our next-door neighbors were from Bailey and Amarillo. We shared stories from all parts of Texas and became fast friends. A boarding student often had to rely on her friends to take the place of family while she away from home and it helped keep her from being lonely. On the other hand, listening to those boarders who didn't have such wonderful home environments made you miss yours all the more.

My mother wrote me at least three times a week, and several of my good friends from Mercedes wrote fairly often. It was not exactly like being in the armed forces, but not all together different, either. We were not allowed to have phones in our rooms, but there was one pay phone in the sitting room at the end of the hall. Of course, conversations were not really private if you used that phone.

The hour or so before "lights out" was spent listening to music, sharing news from home, doing our nails or washing our hair. One night one of the girls (who was always playing jokes on other people) was washing her hair in the first shower stall in the bathroom across the hall. There was a row of sinks adjacent to the shower stall soooo I climbed up on the sink next to where she was, reached over, and started washing her hair with her. It took a minute or two for her to realize there were more than two hands scrubbing her head. Then she let out a scream that made every girl on the whole floor come running. That happened nearly fifty years ago, and it still brings a smile to my face when I think about it.

Friday nights were special at Hockaday. We dressed up for dinner and usually had a wonderful meal. We learned proper etiquette and had a good time doing it. Once a month there was a "birthday night" celebration for all who had a birthday during that particular month and it was great fun, much like a family celebration.

I had always wanted to be a cheerleader in Mercedes (and was, for the 110-pound football team, when I was eleven), but never had the courage to try out for either the junior or varsity cheerleading squads later on. Hockaday, however, didn't have any cheerleaders for its hockey team so I asked if a couple of my friends and I could be the cheerleaders. It wasn't quite the same, but it was fun in its own way.

Doris Day was my movie idol growing up and I always wanted to sing just the way she did. I persuaded my parents to let me take singing lessons and one of the music instructors was kind enough to take the challenge. She spent many hours trying to train my voice, but after a very poor showing at the first recital, she discouraged me from spending any more of my parents' money on lessons. Not all my hopes were dashed, though. Hockaday had a glee club and I tried out for it. Thomas Merriman was the director and a delightful man who oozed music. I shall never forget him as long as I live! He didn't say I had a good voice, but he did say I had the kind of voice that would blend in well with lots of others. Being part of that club was just what I needed. It gave me a sense of being part of the team. We practiced and practiced and practiced. In December, we presented the program at the Christmas Vespers at the Highland Park Presbyterian Church (largest in the United States) to a congregation of several thousand worshipers and later, in the spring, we performed an operetta, "The Red Mill", at one of the local high schools. I had never been part of anything quite so grand and quite so much fun. My singing and dancing were nothing like Doris Day's, but still there I was singing and dancing on stage, quite an accomplishment for a little girl from deep South Texas!

One more special event happened in the spring: Elvis Presley came to town. His performance was held in the Cotton Bowl and he had the teenagers rocking in the aisles. He grabbed the microphone, wiggled his hips, and started singing songs like "Heartbreak Hotel" and "Blue Suede Shoes." By the time he got around to "You Ain't Northing But a Hound Dog," even the elderly chaperones were clapping their hands and patting their feet in time to the beat.

A terrible tornado came through Dallas that year, destroying everything in its path. South Oak Cliff was the hardest hit, and I can still remember listening to the radio and hearing the announcer caution everyone to get to the southeast corner of the room, to stay away from any windows, and to stay calm. It was one of the most terrifying days in my life. I couldn't call home and my family couldn't call me. The sky was black and the winds were whipping the canopy outside my window. You could hear people screaming and crying in the background as the radio station on-the-spot reporters told of seeing homes and buildings completely demolished and dead bodies strewn about in the wake of the storm. I couldn't believe my ears and yet, it was real. All I could do was pray. Thank heaven for prayer!!!

Hockadaisies dressed for church. Boarders wore hats, gloves, and high-heeled shoes every Sunday morning and were bused to various denominations. I attended either the First Presbyterian Church downtown or Highland Park Presbyterian Church. Both were impressive buildings and congregations with huge membership numbers. This was a far cry from the small church I attended in Mercedes, which normally had 40 or 50 members in attendance on Sunday mornings and only a handful of children in the Sunday School classes.

Dr. Billy Graham spoke at one of the Sunday evening services at the downtown church and I was overwhelmed, not only by the words of his sermon, but by his demeanor as well. His words of encouragement, his eagerness to woo people to Christ, and his sense of humor all warmed the cockles of my heart and made me want to be a better Christian. Although I was too "Presbyterian" to accept the altar call that evening, I did leave the sanctuary with a renewed sense of purpose and dedication.

My year at Hockaday was special. The education I received that year was not limited to academics.

Europe with the YMCA Tour

Between my sophomore and junior years, my brother, Bob, and I traveled to Europe on a tour sponsored by the Dallas YMCA. There were nine boys and girls and one chaperone. We flew from Dallas to New York City, and then on to Scotland. As we deplaned, there was a young girl directing us through customs, who was speaking English but we couldn't understand a word she said. She tried to make herself understood, but, in the end, we simply played "follow the leader."

After sight-seeing for several days in Edinburg, we traveled by rail to London. The hotels we stayed in were nice but not plush. Meals were included in the tour and we ate what was prepared for us. There was always a schedule to be followed and everyone had to be accounted for long before departure times.

London was grand! The changing of the guard at Buckingham Palace, Big Ben, Windsor Castle, the Tate Gallery, Madame Tussaud's Wax Museum, the Crown Jewels, St. Paul's Cathedral, and Westminster Abby were but a few of the sights we saw. We toured and we toured. There was one evening set aside for a dinner with some of the local YMCA members and that was fun. We had a chance to get acquainted with people our own age and to learn how teenagers half-way around the world dealt with problems similar to our own. Surprisingly enough, there weren't many differences.

We had our own bus and driver when we sailed from the White Cliffs of Dover to Rotterdam. It was an English coach (with the steering column on the right-hand side) and large enough for everyone to spread out over a couple of seats. It became our home on wheels for the next five weeks.

I remember traveling through Holland and seeing acres and acres of tulips. I was impressed with the windmills and The Hague. We stopped at a souvenir shop where we all dressed in Dutch clothes and wooden shoes and had our photos taken to show the folks back home. It was like a fairy tale.

Germany was full of Gothic cathedrals and I don't think we missed a single one. We did get to go to a biergarten while we were in Munich and it was a night to remember. Lots of our servicemen were stationed there and the band played American songs most of the evening. I had never seen a stein of beer before (except in the movies) and when they placed the rather large mug in front of me, I didn't think I could drink it. However, the more we sang, the more nostalgic I became, and the more I sipped the beer. To say I became rather silly would be an understatement. (I was sure I could sing like Doris Day. Why didn't anyone else think so?)

Our bus broke down in Austria and we had to leave Innsbruck prematurely. We took an overnight train to Italy and twice during the night, the train came to a stop and we were asked to show our passports. That was a little frightening.

It was very early in the morning when we arrived at the railroad station in Venice, but it was already hot and humid. A big dead rat floated in the canal. My first impression of the city was less than stellar. Our hotel was quite small and the rooms were not very comfortable. We spent our two nights there fighting the heat and the bed bugs. St. Mark's Square was the highlight of Venice for me and the gondola ride at night (when everything looked better) was special, too.

We visited Rome for three days and, again, spent all day, every day, seeing the sights: the Fountain of Trevi, the Coliseum, the Sistine Chapel, and the Forum. We were even blessed by Pope Paul II at the Vatican. Huge numbers of people gathered in front of St. Peter's Cathedral in hopes of seeing him and I was impressed by the number of countries represented there. I was unfavorably impressed, however, by the souvenir vendors. I thought it most inappropriate (it reminded me of the money changers in the Bible), until someone suggested that many faithful Catholics bought items such as rosaries or crosses so they could be blessed and taken home to family members and friends. I had to re-think my position.

Bob and I had been given a specific amount of money to spend on our trip and I spent most of mine in Rome. I bought long kid gloves for a couple of girlfriends and bikinis for a couple of others. There was still a little money left in my purse when we headed to Nice, but not much.

The Riviera was unbelievably gorgeous. The turquoise water of the Mediterranean Sea stretched out from the shoreline as far as one could see. It was a short walk from our hotel to the beach and we spent most of the two days we had there in the water or sun-bathing close by. There was plenty to see and plenty to do. You could rent a paddle-boat by the hour or you could watch the locals (who often came for a quick dip) change into their bathing suits right on the beach. Men and women of every age wore bikinis. I was shocked and embarrassed, but I couldn't take my eyes off of them. We seven American girls caught some attention because we were the only ones on the beach in one-piece bathing suits. The fun in the sun was a great reprieve from the many days on the bus, but it did have a down side. Several of us were so sunburned on the backside, we couldn't bend our knees and had to ride on to the Swiss Alps with our legs straight out on the bus seats.

Skiing in Switzerland was an extraordinary experience. We took the train ride up to the Jung Frau and rented ski equipment so everyone could say they had an opportunity to ski the Alps. Neither Bobby nor I had ever been on a pair of skis and were both thrilled at the prospect of taking a lesson. The instructor gave us explicit guidelines to follow as we put on our skis, snow suits, etc. I was surprised at first that our gear included sunglasses, but it didn't take long out on the mountainside to realize the tremendous glare the sun made on the snow. We took short strides and struggled to get our footing. Before I knew it, my brother had taken off. He was headed directly for a cliff and the instructor started yelling at him to fall down. He didn't. We all began screaming and yelling, "Fall down! Bobby, fall down!" He finally heard us and when he did come to a screeching halt, he was only a few feet away from a steep drop off. The instructor cut our lesson short and carefully led us back to the ski lift area.

Paris was our final stop and it was fantastic. Truly, the "City of Lights" was picture-perfect. The Eiffel Tower and the Champs Elysee were unforgettable. The Louvre, the Seine, the artist square at Montmartre, Notre Dame (with the Rose Window), and Napoleon's Tomb were exciting to see as well. There was so much to see and we only had three days to tour the city. One evening we went to a show at the Follies Bergere. Another night we went to the famous Lido de Paris nightclub. Red Skeleton was traveling around the world with his young son who was suffering from a chronic disease, and they were introduced to the audience just before the performance began. The musical production was an extravaganza - beautiful people, fantastic voices, and elaborate costumes (although somewhat skimpy or non-existent in some places). It was an eye opener for me, and I am sure it was a double eye opener for my brother.

Some of the other travelers had placed calls home for additional funds during our travels, but Bobby and I were determined not to exceed the funds we were given at the beginning of the tour. We were quite surprised to learn that there was an airport departure tax and when we made a final accounting of our spending money, we found we had just enough to pay our share. When we landed in New York City, we had only one nickel between the two of us.

Fortunately, our cousin, Eloise Nowak, was there to meet our plane and to give us the money our parents had planned for us to use on our return trip to the Valley. She also gave us the keys to our brother Walt's 1956 Chevrolet convertible. Wow!

Our excursion was not over yet! We drove up to Mt. Holyoke, Massachusetts, to visit our Aunt Eloise (Coffman) for a couple of days. She was still quite a tennis player in her early 60s and we had a great time watching her play at the country club there. There were huge dinosaur tracks left in the granite rock not far from her house and we had fun exploring the sites.

We planned to drive back to spend another night with Cousin Eloise in Saddle Brook, New Jersey (just across the bridge from New York City), and made the mistake of picking up a hitch-hiker in downtown Hartford. He looked a bit like Santa Claus and was very friendly, but when he said he wanted to travel all the way to Texas with us, we told our cousin and she suggested we get out of town before he showed up early the next morning. I remember being on the turnpike to Ft. Wayne long before sunup.

The toll road was quite an experience for both of us. Neither of us was old enough to have a driver's license in some of the northern states so we had to be careful not to get a speeding ticket. Bobby was pleased to find out that the speed limit on the Pennsylvania Turnpike was 80 miles an hour. (Who would want to go any faster than that?) Well, lots of folks left us in their dust. It took us all day (about 600 miles) to reach our destination, but our Aunt Margaret and cousins Mary and Chris Tsiguloff were glad to see us when we arrived in Indiana.

Chris introduced us to Italian pizza. It was loaded with toppings I had never even heard of and we gulped down the whole thing. I met Bobby in the kitchen twice during the night trying to satisfy our thirst for water. Chris had a knowing smile on his face the next morning but never said a word.

St. Louis was our next stop with a visit to friends who had previously lived in Mercedes. I had a crush on the oldest son and their daughter had a crush on Bobby. One evening we took a paddle boat ride down the Mississippi and it was terribly romantic (dinner and dancing beneath a full moon). It could have been a scene from "Showboat."

When we got back to their house about 11:00 o'clock that night, Bobby decided we needed to get in the car and head down to Walter Guy Burkhalter's house in Enid, Mississippi. I was not happy about leaving, but couldn't do much about it. We drove right though an electrical storm. After plowing through some high water areas on the road, we had to pull into a closed gas station in northern Arkansas to let the engine dry out. The zipper in the back of the convertible was open and rain poured into the back seat. Neither of us had anything nice to say for quite a while. When we finally reached our cousin's house as the sun was coming up, we sank into our beds and didn't come out until well past noon.

Bobby wanted to change our plans again and drive right back home to Texas. I had planned all along to go to another cousin's wedding in Columbus, Georgia, and was furious when Bobby said we weren't going. We had a real physical fight; I clawed him with my fingernails and he threw me on the ground. I guess we had had just too much togetherness! Walter Guy came to the rescue and suggested we compromise: Bobby should drive me to the wedding, but as soon as it was over, we should hop in the car and head for home. Neither of us spoke most of the way to Georgia, but we did have a grand time at the wedding. We left shortly after the reception with Bobby in the driver's seat. About 3:00 a.m., he asked me to take a turn at the wheel. I drove for about an hour and couldn't seem to stay awake. Soooo, while he was still sleeping, I stopped at a motel, paid for the room, took the car keys, and gently woke him to say he could either sleep in the motel or the car, it didn't make any difference to me. He grumbled all the way into the motel, but we both needed a rest from the road.

The next day was long. We drove from somewhere in eastern Louisiana to Mercedes in about fourteen hours. Home never looked so good. And Bobby and I were happy to put a little space between ourselves (no, lots of space)!

The Farm Bureau Contest

During my junior year in high school, I represented the City of Mercedes in the Valley Farm Bureau Queen contest and was fortunate enough to be chosen to go to the next level of competition in Corpus Christi for the state title. Mother and I traveled there for the two-day session of events.

The parade of contestants during the luncheon on the first day was not too unsettling because we didn't have to wear bathing suits or anything that revealed one's figure (or lack thereof). I wore a simple white, wool dress with black shoes and a black beret and was given the number seven out of twelve spots in the lineup.

The evening gown competition and the question-and-answer session were, however, of great concern. I spent hours trying to think of what to say to the audience in the time segment allotted to me. I knew precious little about the activities of the Farm Bureau and didn't want to embarrass my parents or myself by my lack of knowledge. My cue cards were still blank at 7:00 that evening when we went on stage for the final event. My contestant number in this event was eleven so I had quite a few more minutes to think about what I might say, but as I listened to the other girls' wonderfully prepared speeches, my heart began to sink. Each one gave a better speech than the one before and there seemed to be nothing left to say. Soooo when they called my name, I said a little prayer, stepped to the center of the stage, thanked them for the privilege of participating in the pageant and told them that my father was a doctor who owned a small orchard. If he needed any advice, he knew he could always call the local Farm Bureau agent. It only took about forty-five seconds.

I don't know if it was the evening gown, the brevity of my speech, or the lucky numbers I had been given but I won the title of Texas State Farm Bureau Queen that night. As soon as Mother and I got back to the hotel, I called home to let my family know and my father said he wasn't surprised, not because he thought I would win but because he had already seen it on television.

I appeared on the local televison news early the next morning and was presented the keys to the City of Corpus Christi, as well as a cowboy hat to take to the mayor of Boston where the national convention was to be held later that year. This was just the beginning of another great adventure.

Mother escorted me on my all-expenses-paid trip to the American Farm Bureau Federation's 40th Annual Convention in Boston in mid-December and it was cold - very, very cold - snow everywhere. We joined other representatives and delegates from Texas at a special meeting in the huge convention center. Ed Dennis of Dimitt, Texas, had won the talent contest at the state convention with his whip-cracking skills, and he was going to be on the program in Boston. He indicated that he needed a target for his whip and guess what? I got the job! Let me tell you that it's one thing to watch someone put a cigarette in his/her mouth and let someone else snap it in two with a whip, and it's another thing to be that person! Again and again, Ed assured me that it was only the sound of the whip and not the actual motion that should concern me. Well, what could I say? Yes, I stood on the stage for about ten minutes while he displayed all his whip-cracking talent. When it was over, I thought it was a rather neat experience but certainly not until it was over.

Texas was going to host the national convention the following year, and it was suggested that the Texas Farm Bureau Queen extend the invitation to everyone in the audience. What? Surely not! Yes, once again I was on the stage. Not only was I to speak to an audience of more than 6000 farmers from around the nation, I was also to appear on the program just before Madame Chiang Kai-shek, the keynote speaker. My heart was in my throat and I could feel the blood racing around in my veins and arteries. Just before I stepped out on the stage, I offered a short prayer and asked for words to say. "Y'all come on down to Texas next year. We'll be waiting for you," was all I could think of and it got a good round of applause, at least from the Texans. It was a marvelous experience; it was a chance of a lifetime; it was time to go home.

A few years later, when I was a college freshman at Southern Methodist University in Dallas, a fellow student said he thought he had heard of me before, "wasn't I the Texas hog-calling queen or something like that?"

Whip-cracker at Farm Bureau Queen Contest.

The Rio Hondo Bridge - 1958

Growing up with brothers just one and two years older, I felt I could do just about anything they could do. I was always willing to take a dare and it got me into trouble on more than one occasion.

Perhaps the most outrageous thing I did as a teenager was to accept a dare to jump off the bridge in Rio Hondo, Texas. A lot of water has passed under the bridge (no pun intended) since I made that decision and some of the details about how/why I decided to do it are vague, but I remember every minute of the actual jump.

I climbed over the side of the bridge to a small platform-like area and stood there for what seemed an eternity. The water was at least 30 or 40 (or maybe 60) feet below and I was beginning to wish I had not taken the dare. Both the boys in our foursome had already dived into the arroyo and were jeering at me because I had only agreed to jump. Well, it took a long time, but I did force myself to step off the platform.

I was in the air a long, long time and only when I hit the water with a great deal of force, did I begin to think I was not going to survive the ordeal. Little did I know what was waiting for me below! I plunged deep into the arroyo, down, down, down, down, down until I hit the murky, muddy bottom. My first fear at this stage was that I was going to be stuck in the muck and never come to the surface. My eyes were open and I could see all kinds of debris (broken glass, beer cans, discarded junk). To me it didn't look like a proper place to die. Prayers came quickly, one right after another, "Please, dear Lord, get me out of this mess and I will be so good!" Slowly I began to swim upwards, pulling with every bit of strength I had. My bathing suit had filled with the awful yucky mud at the bottom and it was weighing me down. It took a very long time for me to reach the surface and a longer time to get the junk out of my bathing suit before I could get out of the water. (One wouldn't want the others to have the last laugh, would one?) Did I mention the smell at the bottom of the arroyo when I stirred up the muck? Guess that's better left to your imagination.

This story has made me well known in some circles. I have often been referred to as that crazy girl from Mercedes who jumped off the Rio Hondo bridge. (Even my oldest granddaughter has told her teenage friends about it.)

Hawaii

After high school graduation Margie Collier, Charlene Traylor, and I went to the University of Hawaii in 1959 for the first semester of summer school. I flew from Dallas to San Francisco to spend a few days with my aunt and uncle before getting on the ship to Hawaii. It was 95 degrees when I left Texas but only 46 degrees when I arrived in California. I had on a cotton dress and was amazed to see ladies in fur coats in the airport when we landed. The climate difference was just one item in the culture shock I experienced. There was so much to see and so little time to see it: the Golden Gate Bridge, Chinatown, Fisherman's Wharf, Alcatraz, and the Pacific Ocean (everything one saw in the movies and more). There was even a farewell celebration at the pier as our ship pulled out to sea, complete with streamers and band music. It was so exciting.

The first day on board was spent hugging the coastline because we were only sailing down to Los Angeles to pick up the rest of the five hundred girls traveling with us. The waters were rough and I spent most of the day in my tiny room wishing I felt better than I did. Things didn't get any better as we sailed away to Hawaii. Our room was on the next to bottom deck and although we couldn't open the porthole, I am sure we would have seen lots of fish if we could have. We had to climb several staircases to get to the fresh air and none of us made it during the first twenty-four hours. We existed on crackers and water. To add to our misery, there was a dormitory-style room just across the hall from us with lots of people, all happily talking and singing. We couldn't even suffer in silence!

Day two was much better. Once we got to the fresh air, we stayed there. The tour had planned activities for us and there were lots of fun choices. My favorite activity was just being able to breathe in and breathe out, without the sense of nausea. We enjoyed the next couple of days and were really getting our "sea legs" when we arrived in Honolulu. There was a reception committee awaiting us and it was (again) just like in the movies. Girls in hula skirts greeted each of us with a lei while someone played the ukelele in the background. The white sand beaches were beautiful and Diamond Head stood majestically in the distance. (Wow! I thought we had a great beach at South Padre Island, but this was unbelievably gorgeous.) The water was aqua and so clear you could easily see the coral reef below the surf. There were some mighty good-looking guys on the beach as well. I can't remember how many young men serving in the military were stationed on the island of Oahu, but someone said the ratio was twenty-five guys to a girl - not bad numbers!

The university dormitory we stayed in was a men's dorm during the regular school year and didn't have many of the privacy features some of us would have preferred. The shower was one long area with no curtains in between, and only a number of the commode stalls had doors. The girls with great bodies didn't seem to mind if they had to share these areas, but I did. I scheduled my showers when no one else was around.

My class in World Civilization began at 8:00 am. I actually made it to class most days, but I can't say I was overly enthusiastic about the course. The textbook was huge and jam-packed with information I could hardly absorb so early in the morning. However, by the time I got to the hula dancing class at 10:00, I seemed to be able to pay more attention. What great fun! We bought grass skirts, wore leis, and learned how to tell stories with our hands and hips. This was truly an education. Who cared about academics?

By noon every day we were on our way to Waikiki Beach. We had to walk down the hill to the main street and take a ten-minute bus ride to the hotel area where all the girls spent their afternoons tanning, surfing, and looking for movie stars.

Margie had a eye for famous people; she could spot them a mile away. She was the first to see Ricky Nelson, Loretta Young, and David Niven. We were walking through the International Marketplace one evening when she saw Mr. Niven. She ran toward him, yelling and motioning for me to hurry up and join her so we could get his autograph. I was reluctant to bother him and didn't want to be a nuisance, but he was very gracious; he gave us each a kiss as well as his signature. We talked about that for years!

Another highlight was a two-day trip to the Big Island. The tour included souvenir shopping in the capital city of Hilo, a luau beside a fresh water pool with floating orchids, and a bus trip around the whole island with stops at the black sand beaches and a close-up view of the smoldering volcanos. This was certainly paradise and so romantic that I decided not to go back until I was married. (Margie lost her billfold on the Big Island but that's another story.)

During our last week of summer school, the entire group of five hundred girls from Texas and California was asked to pose on the campus for the centerfold of "Life" magazine. About mid-morning we gathered in the common area, and waited for the photographer to arrive. After the first thirty minutes or so, I felt a little sick to my stomach. My head ached and my palms were sweaty. There wasn't a restroom close by so I decided to just make the best of it and do nothing. Well, after another thirty minutes or so, Mother Nature took over and I dashed to the first building I could find. I looked for the ladies' room but it was on the second floor and I didn't think I could make that. There was a men's restroom right in front of me and no one was in sight, soooo I ducked in and threw up right in the first commode. I was silently praying no one would come in or out while I was there. Thank heaven no one did. I felt much better then and returned to the photo area just in time to be included in the picture. I can't remember which issue our photo appeared in, but I am sure Margie still has a copy.

Our tour of Pearl Harbor was one of the most heart-rending experiences I have ever known. A young man in uniform was our tour guide and he told the story of the Japanese invasion with such emotion and expression, we couldn't keep the tears from streaming down our faces. We felt a part of the history that took place that day in 1941 and our hearts ached for all those who were lost in battle and their families as well. The tour only lasted a few hours; the impression it made on me has lasted a lifetime.

When it came time to return to the mainland, Margie and I were happy to be traveling by plane, or so we thought. There was engine trouble on our scheduled flight so we waited twelve hours for the next plane to Los Angeles. Of course we missed our original flight from L.A. to Dallas and the connecting one to San Antonio. Our mothers were supposed to be waiting for us at the airport, but when we finally arrived, neither mother was there. We tried calling the hotel but neither mother was in her room. Soooo, we jumped into a taxi and rode to the hotel. We found her mom, just coming out of the dining room, but my mother had gone with my sister to see "South Pacific" at a local theater. What a blow! One would have thought they would have been searching high and low for us, but, no, they just went right on living! I couldn't stand it. I knew my mother couldn't be enjoying some movie while I was missing. That was a preposterous idea. I jumped into another taxi, got to the movie theater just before intermission, and found Eloise and Mother having a splendid evening together. They did seem somewhat happy to see me, but they were celebrating Eloise's birthday and they were quite content to tell me all about the wonderful show. Mother did say later on that evening that when the airlines told her not to expect us for at least twelve hours, she didn't see any reason not to go ahead and enjoy the time she had to wait. How could I argue with that? She was always so very practical!

We sped back to the Valley the next morning. It was always so good to get home and we only had a few weeks to get ready for college.

College Friends and Events

Four years of fun and laughter? Well, yes and no! Freshman Rush for girls took place the first week in September at Southern Methodist University in Dallas. It was supposed to be a wonderful time filled with parties and activities, and, for me, it was grand. I was the perfect candidate for sorority life. The bond of sisterhood was just what I needed to help me through the first year of life on campus. Immediately there were 60 or more girls who cared about you. Your grades were important, your social life was important, and your adjustment to college life was important. There was an entire family of people willing to share your concerns. It was extra-special for me!

Of course, there were some girls who didn't uphold all the ideals of the sorority, but there were plenty of others who went way beyond the call of sisterhood and set admiral examples for others to follow. We played lots of bridge, watched soap operas together, and shared our lives for four years. There were plenty of laughs and quite a few tears.

Champ Jones and I began dating at the end of my sophomore year in college. He was a strong-willed, somewhat cocky guy, who expected immediate success in having a romantic relationship with me. I, on the other hand, resisted any authority he thought he had over my life. (It took him more than two years to convince me to marry him.)

Spring Break was dreadful. I had asked several of my sorority sisters to come to the Valley for a vacation at South Padre only to find Champ had also invited some of his fraternity brothers. We met up with them at South Padre and made plans for an evening in Mexico. Champ was pleased with the arrangements, but his friends bailed out on him at the last minute soooo he had the pleasure of five girls' company, instead of the one he intended. (It took me quite a few years to see the lighter side of this episode.)

My senior year I decided to travel to Austin to see my sister and her family. Champ didn't think I should drive there by myself so he traveled along with me. I explained that I didn't really need a chaperone and could manage the trip by myself, but he insisted he should come along.

After dropping him off at the SAE fraternity house, I went to visit my good friend, Donnie Vollmer, who was living in Kinsolving dormitory. We spoke on the phone and she gave me directions to her room on the second floor. I was not familiar at all with the University of Texas campus, but thought I could follow her directions and get by to see her. Wrong!!!! I drove up to the building, hopped out of my car, and walked up the sidewalk and up the staircase before I realized I might be in the wrong place. There were several men on the first floor (not too uncommon in a women's dorm), but no one but men on the second floor. Some of those men had towels; others didn't! I couldn't get back down those stairs fast enough!!! By that time, some of the guys on the first floor of the fraternity house had followed me up the stairs. It was difficult getting past them on my way out, without saying who I was or why I was there. I don't remember giving them any personal information, but I do remember they were laughing uncontrollably as I ran out the front door. It was only about half a block to Kinsolving. I made it there in record time.

There were several SAE fraternity brothers Champ was close to at SMU, but Dick Hull was one of the most colorful. We double-dated quite often. Dick was (and is to this day) one of my best friends as well as Champ's. Our friendship has survived four decades of escapades and adventures. He has been a blessing in our lives and a real challenge as well.

After double-dating to a SMU football game and taking Dick's date home, we drove back to the Chi Omega sorority house. Dick thought it would be nice to let Champ and me have a few minutes to "say" goodnight, so he got out of Champ's car and crawled up on the one next to it. Well, after Champ walked me to the front door and returned to the car, he forgot all about Dick and drove away. Dick must have fallen asleep waiting for us to kiss goodnight and was most surprised when he awoke a couple of hours later without a ride home. He was not a happy fellow.

One of the most difficult times I had at SMU was dealing with the "God is Dead" issue on campus during my sophomore year. I was taken aback by such thoughts. Everyone I knew growing up in Mercedes had gone to church. I couldn't believe so many people actually thought that God was not alive and not in control. It was contrary to everything I trusted! I listened, but was never convinced. My whole life experience told me something quite different: God was alive and well in my life! I needed to share that with others. Oh, no, I wasn't going to get on some soapbox on the corner and shout it out to passers-by. No, I was going to live a life that said it through expressions of love and concern for others. I took classes in religion which gave me a perspective of the faith found in other cultures, and it gave me a deep appreciation for them as well as my own. I debated religious/social issues in the classroom, and began to recognize how little I knew about the things I thought I knew very well. My degree in religion was just the beginning of my adult faith journey.

Our Wedding and Honeymoon

When I called home in September to tell my parents that Champ and I were engaged, my father was a little surprised I was going to marry a boy from Donna (only eight miles down the road). He asked why I hadn't just married him right after high school graduation, and saved him all the money he had to spend on my education at SMU. I assured him that I needed the education to fall back on in case the marriage didn't turn out well.

The ceremony took place in Dallas, in the chapel of the Highland Park Presbyterian Church, on December 21, 1963. (My father later noted that it was the longest night of the year. I had to agree). There were nearly 150 guests at the church, but quite a few more at the reception at the downtown City Club. The champagne flowed. All the while we were taking pictures and cutting the cake, the champagne flowed. When the formalities were over, I spent quite a bit of time changing into my "going away" outfit. The Scottish nature of my father began to surface when several addi-

Honeymoon Beginning.

tional cases of wine were brought in for guest consumption, and he sent a quick message to me in the ladies' dressing room to get changed and get out the door. It only took a few more minutes, but I did have time for a few last laughs with my attendants before I appeared. Champ was waiting (patiently, I am sure) with a bottle of champagne tucked under his arm and a smile on his face. Rice flew in our direction, and we were out the door and into the night. It was snowing! How very romantic!

We headed to the Valley by car the next morning. Traveling in the snow was tedious and slow. (Champ had lost his smile of the previous evening.) I thought it was great fun to slip and slide around, but he didn't agree. It took several hours to get to Waco on the icy highway, but then the road conditions improved considerably. We managed to get to Champ's parents' home just after dark. Of course, no one was there (they were back in Dallas), and we had the whole place to ourselves. Imagine my delight! Here we were seven miles out in the country with nobody around - nobody. I wasn't exactly scared, but I had always lived in either a two-story house or a dormitory with the bedrooms on the second floor. I had never heard such noises: bushes brushing up against the window screens, coyotes howling in the distance, and Champ droning on and on about his high school and college football achievements. It was almost more than a body could take!

The next couple of days we spent visiting with friends and relatives and getting ready for Christmas. We played lots of bridge at my parents' house and enjoyed watching bowl games on television.

One afternoon we took my brother-in-law, Joe Galvan, out to the ranch to hunt dove. Unfortunately for me, the men killed 35 birds. We took them to back to the house and began plucking them. Yuck! That was bad enough, but they had to be gutted as well! Double yuck! It was my first and last time to do that. (I have cooked many a dove, white-wing, or quail since then, but I have left the field preparation to someone else.)

After spending Christmas day with my family, we drove to New Orleans for the real honeymoon. You know, the part you dream about - strolling around Jackson Square, dunking beignets in café a lait at the Café du Monde, and wining and dining at the famous restaurants. Well, it was nothing like that! It snowed and it snowed. It had not snowed in New Orleans at that time for more than 30 years, but it snowed and it snowed. We spent most of our time in the hotel room. What else could we do in such inclement weather?

My cousin Walter Guy (you remember him, don't you?) and a whole host of his buddies were in town for the Sugar Bowl, and took us down to Bourbon Street the night before the Ole Miss game. He suggested we should take in a strip tease act. Guy thought it would be a good education for me. It would BROADen my horizons, if you will. He was right! Although it was a new experience for me and one I didn't relish, I did come away with a greater appreciation for the art of tassel-twirling than I had ever known before.

We cut our stay in New Orleans a day short, partly because we were running out of money and partly because it was continuing to snow (if you get my drift). The decision to leave was made rather hastily and by the time we got to Texas, it was well into the night. I reached into my overnight kit for something and cut my thumb on Champ's razor. It bled quite a bit, but there wasn't anything to do but put a make-shift bandage on it. We wrapped it tightly in Kleenex and drove on toward his brother's house in Houston. The gas tank was almost empty when we got to Galveston, but Champ was sure we could make it all the way (another 90 miles). I was a nervous wreck. My thumb was throbbing and I wanted to stop and find a place to sleep. Champ kept driving. Shortly after 3:00 a.m. we arrived at Larry and Helen's house. Thank heaven! I couldn't wait to get out of the car. Champ, however, wouldn't let me disturb them. He said that they would be getting up to go to work before long and we should just sit and wait for their lights to come on. Soooo, we sat in the car in the driveway for just over two hours. ("Happy honeymoon, honey!" Isn't that what my mother had said as we left home just a few days ago? I was trying to have a happy honeymoon - really I was.) When the lights finally came on, we went inside and removed the bandage from my thumb. I nearly fainted as they carefully tried to pull the tissue from my tissue. Larry and Helen went to work and we fell into bed.

The drive back to Dallas was uneventful, but I think we both agreed that we had had all the honeymooning we could take.

The Wedding in Baton Rouge

A close fraternity brother of Champ's, Joe Ted Davidson, was planning to get married in Baton Rouge and most of our friends were planning to drive the 500 miles there from Dallas. I couldn't go because I worked Saturdays until 3:00 p.m. The closer the time came to the wedding, the more excited our friends' conversations became about what fun they were going to have and the more dejected I felt. However, there was absolutely no way I could ask to have the day off. I had been off for two weeks for my own wedding just a couple of months before.

I tried not to let my disappointment show too much, but the Friday they left was a long, miserable day for me. The hours dragged by at the office and the evening alone (while the others were partying at the rehearsal dinner) made matters worse. In the middle of the night, the thought came to me that I could find a way to get there if I just put my mind to it. I called the airlines and found a flight that would arrive just about the time of the wedding and I booked it. I called Mike Schmidt, a very good friend who lived in our apartment complex, and asked him if he would be kind enough to take me to the airport. He listened to my plan of surprising Champ and then was very quiet. He wondered out loud if it was a good idea. He thought I might want to reconsider my trip. He wasn't sure Champ would be pleased to be surprised (might be having a good time with one of the bridesmaids - ha! ha! - just kidding). I was crushed! It never occurred to me that Champ wouldn't be glad to see me. Still, I had to find out for myself. Mike finally agreed to take me to the airport but he gave me every opportunity to change my mind on the way there.

In order to arrive at the reception in the proper attire, I had to get on the plane in a dressy evening suit so I had to cover myself with some type of wrap that would be fairly attractive and yet practical. I finally decided on a reversible poncho which had large pockets on both sides. I stuffed my nightgown into one pocket and undies, etc. in another. I pinned my clothes for traveling home into the back of the poncho and used the last two pockets for my shoes, toothbrush and other toiletries. I didn't have to walk into the reception carrying a suitcase; I was wearing one!

Once I got on the plane and had time to reflect on Champ's possible reaction, I began to feel sick at my stomach. Why did I think he would be so thrilled to see me? What if he was having a good time without me? What if? By the time the plane landed, I was a almost in tears. Should I fly back to Dallas right that minute or should I go to the reception and face the music? I prayed for help, and then decided there was no going back.

As the taxi drove up to the reception hall, I could see some of our friends gathered together just outside the front door. When they saw me drive up in the taxi, one of them went in to tell Champ I was there. He came out with a big smile on his face. Hallelujah!!! He hugged and kissed me, and said my being there was a wonderful surprise. Hallelujah, once again.

The young lady checking coats was a bit startled by the weight of my poncho, but a broad smile came over her face as she discovered its contents. Then she carefully placed it on a hanger next to one of the more elegant evening wraps.

I enjoyed the rest of the trip more than anyone else and after a while, I did actually forgive Mike for planting that seed of doubt, but I haven't forgotten it.

The Dallas Wedding

Peggy Golden was one of my dearest friends during my years at SMU. She visited our home in Mercedes on more than one occasion and I very often spent time in her home in Dallas. Her lifestyle was quite different from mine, but we had lots of fun together. Her father was a prominent attorney (President of the Dallas Bar Association at one time) and her mother was the epitome of a Dallas socialite. She served on numerous civic boards and committees, and was also active in a great many community and church activities. The family's weekly calendar was cluttered with social engagements.

After graduation from college, Peggy made her debut and she invited me to all of the parties where she was being honored. I was thrilled, but my father wasn't. Clothes for these events cost big bucks, and I really had to do some serious convincing when it came down to the fox stole I thought I had to have for the actual coming-out ball. It was like being in a movie for me - partying with beautiful people in beautiful houses with absolutely fabulous food and music. It was wonderful fun.

Peggy was one of the bridesmaids in our wedding and I was a bridesmaid in hers. Our wedding was in the chapel of the Highland Park Presbyterian Church with about 150 guests in attendance and hers took place in Highland Park Methodist Church with five times that many guests. We married on December 21st and she married six months later, to the day. I had four attendants and she had thirteen. My bridesmaids wore royal blue gowns and hers wore gowns of seven different pastel shades, resembling the colors found in a rainbow.

Thank Heaven for Laughter

What I remember most about her wedding was actually getting dressed for the event. The floor-length lavender gown I was going to wear was simply gorgeous and I felt like Cinderella in it. It wasn't until I was ready to walk out the door that Champ took a look at me and said I couldn't go out like that. The dress was lined but the material was so sheer, he could see my girdle right through the skirt. Did I want to walk down that aisle and have everyone see what he could see? Of course, I didn't. What was I going to do? No one I knew had a long slip and there was no time to go out and buy one. Soooo, I cut up a pillow case and stood on a chair and turned around in a circle while Champ used safety pins to attach the pillow case to the bottom of my short slip. (I hope you can envision that.) I could hardly keep from falling off the chair myself! My macho, football-player husband had never done anything like that before, but he saved the day that night. When I arrived at the church, I noticed several of the other bridesmaids had the same see-through problem I had, but there wasn't time to do anything about it. Thank heaven for Champ! (I have, on more than one occasion.)

Part Two - Special Events

Moving to Donna

Right before Champ graduated from The Southern Methodist School of Law, he informed me that he had decided to go to work for an attorney in Donna after he passed the Bar examination. The news was not well-received! I had always thought we would be staying in Dallas and had envisioned plans for a lifetime in "Big D." I cried and I cried but to no avail!

We moved to "Little D" in July of 1965 and rented a house right next door to "Mean Jo Green" (that's what the children called her when she wasn't in sight). Jo had a rather husky voice and was quick to voice her thoughts about every situation. She said what she thought and meant what she said, and she was willing to put up her dukes, if necessary. I knew right away I wanted to be her friend and not her enemy. We started out as neighbors but ended up as lifelong friends.

After three short months, Champ decided that he wasn't working enough to justify the $300 salary he was earning soooo he gave notice and quit his job. I was horrified! My job as a secretary at the Comptroller's Office didn't pay nearly that much, and we had rent to pay as well as other living expenses. He said he thought he could open an office at the back of the Donna Office Building and work for himself.

The first month he grossed $60 and $25 of that went to pay the rent. He could only afford to pay his secretary $1.25 an hour for one or two hours a day, and she had to bring her portable typewriter with her. Fortunately, we had a friend, Carol King Farris, who was willing to come when he needed secretarial help. He didn't need anyone most of the time. No, most of his time was spent visiting with either his dad or one of his dad's friends. (There were not a lot of folks beating on his door the first couple of months.) To make matters worse, his small office space was adjacent to the lavatory and you could hear every time the commode was flushed, not exactly an auspicious beginning to Champ's legal career.

He did, however, find a good job for me! The Donna Independent School District had implemented a new program for migrants. It was geared to those students who traveled to the mid-west and north to pick vegetables and fruit in the fields during the late spring and summer months. Classes, beginning in early November, were held for only six months (instead of nine), but the children were in the classroom from 8:00 a.m. until 5:00 p.m. It looked good on paper, but it was a rigorous schedule for all of us involved in the program. The best part of the position was the pay, $400 a month. Wow! I had never considered teaching as a career, but how could I say no to that amount of money?

Champ had an offer for an attorney's position in New York City later that year which paid almost a $1,000 a month. It sounded good at first, but the more we discussed the possibility of moving to the "Big Apple", the more content I realized I was in "Little D". Again I cried and cried; this time it worked! Donna was going to be our home forever.

We owned precious little furniture when we arrived in Donna. I think we had a lamp and a couple of small tables, but nothing of any consequence. Our parents were kind enough to help us furnish our small rented house with what we called "early relative" pieces. None of them were akin (ha! ha!) to each other, but all of them were appreciated.

Our first major purchase was a living room couch and we had to pay top dollar for it. If I remember correctly, it cost about $500, which was more than our combined monthly salaries. However, it proved to be well worth the investment as it still sits in our living room today. (Oh, the stories it could tell!)

Thank Heaven for Laughter

It was a turquoise sectional sofa with 13 cushions made of durable fabric. It could easily seat seven people or sleep two adults. It could fit into a corner and still fill up a room. It was just what we needed to make our little house a home.

We took it with us when we moved south of town to the old family home about seven miles out in the country. A few years later, when we moved back into town, we had it re-covered and it became the focus of our new family room. In fact, we designed the room around that one large piece of furniture.

Our three sons loved that couch as they were growing up. They often made forts or hideouts with the cushions and jumped endless hours on the springs (when Champ wasn't looking). They liked to crawl over the half-wall in the kitchen and slide down onto the cushions. They used the cushions to make a train track or a battle ship. Their imaginations ran wild. On rainy days, it was a lifesaver for little boys who had lots of energy and couldn't go outside to play.

Our grandchildren still love to rearrange the cushions and seldom visit our home without creating something new with them. Not long ago they made a "secret place" underneath the baby grand piano in the living room and invited me to come in and have a look around. I managed to get down on the floor and crawl in, but as soon as I did, they wanted to do something else. They tore down the cushion walls and went off to play in another room. I sat there awhile smiling to myself. Fortunately, "Candid Camera" was not in the neighborhood.

Family on the Patio in Donna.

That piece of furniture has been restored and/or re-covered

four times over the years. We have even considered getting rid of it, but there is just too much history and too much family enjoyment left in it to let it go.

Donna has always had a wonderful football tradition, and won the State Championship in 1961. For years, people recognized the town by the accomplishments of its teams. Today, Donna doesn't enjoy the same good reputation it once had, but the vast majority of the townspeople are still good people and it is still a good place to raise children.

One of the nicest features of living in a small community, like Donna, is that you get to be friends with people a few years older than you and a few years younger. Then their children become friends of your children. The bond of friendship extends for generations and they seem more like family than friends. We have been blessed to share our lives with the Farrises, the Villegases, the Greens, the Adames, the Fasanos, the Persons, the Bells, the Armoras, the Guinns, the Todds, and many more.

Hunting in Texas

White-Wing Dove Hunts

My introduction to bird hunting back in the late 60's was pleasant enough. It was fun to be part of the annual white-wing dove hunt which took place the first two weekends in September. Champ was so anxious for me to participate, he bought me a 24 gauge shotgun for my birthday. (What a sweetheart!)

Everyone would congregate in a field down near the Rio Grande River and pick out a spot to set up camp. Although the birds rarely flew before mid to late afternoon, all the hunters were in place shortly after noon so they could spend time with their friends, talk about how good or bad the previous year's hunt was, have a beer or two and discuss the weather. The women seldom went along, but always packed plenty of good groceries for the men and children. Even if there were no birds to speak of, the afternoon wasn't a complete waste because one could always enjoy the food.

The early afternoon hours were usually very hot and still. Waiting for the time to pass was less than exciting, but every now and then a single bird would appear in the sky and five shotguns would aim at it. If the bird fell, several hunters might claim it. If it managed to fly by unscathed, excuses and snide remarks were heard up and down the field. It was fascinating to watch some of the more skilled shooters drop their targets just feet from where they were standing. Their expertise in determining the flight pattern and speed of the bird was praiseworthy, and it made their need for a hunting dog unnecessary.

Champ was a fairly good shot and could get his fair share of the birds, but he had difficulty in seeing where they landed. It was poor sportsmanship not to make every effort to pick up the fallen birds so I came to his rescue and became his "retriever." It sounds a little demeaning, but that was not the case. I found lots of birds that would have otherwise been left for the ants (or worse) and it gave me something to do to help pass the time. The shotgun I owned had a rather tinny (ping, ping) sound when it was shot, not the boom of the 12 gauges, and I was happy to leave it on the rack in the pickup.

When our three sons came along, they joined in the fun of the hunt as well. At first they played in or around the pickup with some of the other children; then they graduated to having their own BB guns; then, about the age of 8, they got their first shotguns. By the time they were teenagers, they could shoot with the best of them and seldom came home without their limits. (Fortunately for me, they could see well enough to retrieve their own birds.)

Champ still goes through the motions of preparing for the dove hunt each September, but he doesn't have to be at "his spot" as early as he used to and he doesn't have to stay as long as he did. Also he's not quite as disappointed if he doesn't get his limit, but he still enjoys the camaraderie.

Deer Hunting in Starr County

In 1967, Champ and I spent one night in November with his parents and their friends, Beryl and Stanford "Home Brew" Todd, at a deer lease just north of Rio Grande City. The camp consisted of two travel trailers, a small one-room building, and a cook shack with a pot-bellied stove.

We stayed in the smallest trailer and there I had my first close encounter with a mouse. I opened the chest of drawers to put away my clothes, and a mouse jumped right into my face. I screamed, it squealed, and the race was on to get out of that trailer. Champ came running, but was disappointed that it was only a mouse that had scared me. He thought it must have been a rattler or something worse. Well, I didn't open that drawer again. I put my things back in the suitcase and hoped for the time to pass quickly so we could go home.

The cook shack was the gathering place for meals and visiting around the stove on cold nights. It was interesting to listen to the stories the men told of that day's hunting experiences as well as those of times gone by. Each one seemed to have a story better than the one before, and the evening wore away without notice. Only when it was time to turn in did I recall the mouse experience. I really didn't think I would be able to sleep a wink and I was right. There must have been a family of mice in that drawer. I didn't look!

Bright and early we were up and having coffee. The deer hunters had gone to their blinds before daylight and would be returning before long.

Although they didn't come home with a buck, they had each seen one or two and were anxious for the afternoon hunt. They were always looking for "Butch", the elusive trophy deer, the bully of the woods, and no one knew when he just might step out into a sendero.

Between deer hunts there was always time for quail hunting excursions. Brew was famous for his "skillet shots" (when a covey of birds stayed in a huddle and six, seven, or more could be killed with a single shell), and seldom came home empty-handed. He was also a very good cook. He enjoyed steaming quail until the meat fell off the bone and he took pride in the gravy he made. He very often stirred the gravy for an hour or more, not because it improved the gravy, but because it allowed him a little more time to enjoy his drink.

The fresh air, the good company, and the good conversation made up for the scary little mention of the snake skin someone had found on the kitchen shelf, and I considered the whole venture a worthwhile experience. LITTLE DID I KNOW HOW MUCH MY LIFE WOULD MIRROR THIS WEEKEND.

Our First Lease

Charles Farris, Andrew Champion, and Champ leased a piece of land just seven miles north of Brew's place the following year and pulled two trailers up there to make camp. The 850 acres were easy to get around, but the entrance road was terribly muddy most of the hunting season, and the ruts were extremely deep. It was almost impassable.

The joggling and juggling on the road was almost too much for any of us, but it was most difficult for my mother. She had heard us talking about our hunting camp adventures and said she would like to see the lease soooo we asked her to come along. It took about 45 minutes to get from the paved highway to our trailer and she never complained a minute. When we accepted Brew's invitation and drove back to his camp for dinner, she never complained a minute. When we drove back over that same road to our camp to spend the night, she never complained a minute. When we got home the next day, she took me aside and said I was a better wife than she had ever given me credit for.

Our lease had its share of mice and you could often hear them running around in the attic of our trailer. (Charlie's trailer had them everywhere. They didn't even try to hide.) We had scorpions and rattlesnakes, and coyotes howling in the dark. We had dirt and sand blowing in the air. We had hot days and hot nights (even in the winter), and we had a baby boy along to share in all the fun.

Mike was not quite two when we first introduced him to hunting and now, at 37, he still loves it. He learned several lessons at that tender age: you don't tinkle into the wind; you don't tinkle on rocks; and you can sleep without a pacifier. He willingly accepted any lack of his creature comforts.

I wonder if my lifestyle would have changed much if he had hated it, but I won't ever know. All my boys have enjoyed hunting throughout the years and now their children are enjoying it as well. It has been the one recreation we could do as a family.

Champ killed his biggest deer at this lease and has aimed at quite a few since then. He decided long ago, however, he wouldn't kill another buck unless it was bigger than the first, so most of the harvesting has been done by the boys. We had the antlers mounted as a reminder of that place and the great times we had there.

The Brock Estate

A few years later, twelve men from Donna decided to lease the Brock Estate ranch on the road to La Gloria, Texas, which was famous for the size of its deer and the size of its snakes. The campsite was quite impressive with its many travel trailers and campers, but the rattlesnake skins hanging on the entrance fence caught my eye immediately. There were at least eight skins, each about six feet long. Did Champ really think this was a good place to let our little boys play while he hunted deer? I couldn't sleep that first night, for sure. The next day we saw trails in the sand where huge snakes had moved right through the center of the camp during the nighttime hours. I was horrified and wanted desperately to pick up my marbles (kids) and go home. Somehow Champ convinced me that wouldn't happen again and I stayed, but my eyes were glued to the ground.

I was walking over to have coffee with Virginia Hearn one afternoon and turned around to see why Matthew (age two) wasn't right behind me. He was several feet back and a large black tarantula was crawling up the front of his yellow jumpsuit. I screamed, he cried, and I descended on the spider in a flash. With one slap of the hand, it went sailing off Matthew's chest. I grabbed him up in my arms and ran to tell Virginia what had happened. When Champ returned to camp a few hours later, I told him every little detail of my heroic gesture, and he replied that although our son might have gotten sick from a possible bite, he probably wouldn't have died. (I still have my doubts.)

Sitting in the deer blind with two small boys was not ideal for any of us. First of all, we had to get them up, dressed, and fed before daylight. We had to get to our blind and then we had to get into our blind. That was no easy process! The boys had a hard time being quiet any time, but particularly when we insisted they be. The opening of the blind windows always made a great noise. After we got everyone situated, we would sit quietly but nothing would happen. We didn't see anything; we didn't hear anything. About the time the sun was coming up, one of the boys would have to tinkle and we would have to open the squeaky blind door. Champ often grew impatient with the boys and me, but I really think his frustration was with the lack of game we saw. We were always delighted to see the green jays and once in a great while, a small doe would make an appearance in the sendero, not exactly the big deer hunter's dream.

My mom kept the boys for us one week night and Champ and I took off to the deer lease to kill the trophy deer while everyone else was at work. Ha! Ha! We had a pleasant evening and set our clock for about 5:00 a.m. Champ had seen a nice buck and wanted a real opportunity to get him soooo we were up and out the door shortly after five. Unfortunately for us, the pickup didn't start. No matter how hard he tried, Champ could not get the engine to turn over. He was not going to miss this chance to kill "Butch" so we walked about a mile to the blind. Champ was walking ahead of me and I had to hurry every little bit to catch up to him. I was carrying a very large pipe in my hand (in case I had a snake encounter), and it rather slowed me down. We managed to get to the blind just before daylight, and when the sun came out, a stately buck stuck his head out of the brush just 100 yards from us. I was just as excited as Champ was and kept saying over and over again,"Hurry up! He isn't going to stay there all day." Champ carefully aimed his rifle, took a deep breath, pulled the trigger, and nothing happened. He couldn't believe it. I couldn't believe it. "What happened," I asked? It took only a few minutes for him to figure it out. Someone had borrowed his gun and had taken the shell out of the chamber. It was not loaded. The walk back to the trailer was longer than I care to remember.

We had some really good times with our friends at this lease because of the sheer numbers. Where else would one cook ten dozen eggs for breakfast or grill thirty or forty pork chops for dinner? Where else would there be so many hunters waiting their turn to tell you their "Butch" tales?

The Hill County Lease

Champ and his brothers bought some property near Fredericksburg, Texas, back in the mid 70's and we made it our new hunting home. The six-hour drive from the Valley was long, but well worth the time it took to get there. The scenery was beautiful and the game was plentiful, not large but plentiful. In fact, when we spread corn out in the front yard, the deer came by the dozens to get their share of the bounty. You could actually sit up in bed, look out your bedroom window first thing in the morning, and see the pecking order amongst the deer unfolding. The larger does shooed away the smaller ones, the more aggressive does shooed away the shyer does and young bucks, and the big bucks shooed away the mean does. They often reared up on their hind legs and kicked at one another, and they often bared their teeth in a snarling gesture. What fun to watch nature up close and personal.

There was a huge man-made pond on the front portion of the property where the boys enjoyed swimming and turtle shooting. There was lots of space in the back 80 acres for exploring and camping out. Matthew was particularly fond of fending for himself in the wild and often set off for an adventure by himself. I insisted he wear a red cap so I could keep track of his whereabouts and he did (most of the time).

Another Mouse Episode

As we were up early one morning getting ready for one of our many trips to the Hill Country, Mitchell, age six, came running out of his bedroom saying he had seen a mouse in the bathroom. No one believed him or took the time to go to look, so he took matters into his own hands and decided to kill the mouse himself.

The mouse was still cowering in the corner when Mitchell returned to the bathroom. Mitch grabbed the plunger and began his attack. The mouse raced over the floor, up over one of his boots and straight up Mitchell's pant leg. He shrieked, the mouse squealed, and Mitchell caught it just inches away from his most private area. Not knowing what to do next, he limped (like Chester of "Gunsmoke") into the kitchen with his hand clutching his groin, and told us what had happened. What a dilemma! He didn't want to let go of the critter, but he wasn't anxious to squeeze it to death, either. Champ remarked that he only had one of those two choices to make; Mitchell opted for the latter.

I guess most families don't have mouse stories, but ours seems to have quite a few.

Thanksgiving Lunch in the Snow

I'll never forget the one Thanksgiving we celebrated there in 1979. Champ, his mother, and Mitchell had gone up a few days early to make preparations for the big day while I stayed home in order to bring the older boys up after they got out of school Wednesday afternoon. Champ had invited some friends over for Thanksgiving dinner and there were going be about twenty of us for the noon meal. Our mobile home had a fairly good-sized kitchen and I always enjoyed cooking for a crowd, but I didn't know the weather would play such a role in the day's events.

It snowed several times that week and my boys were thrilled at the thought of seeing and playing in the snow. We no sooner got there than the bowl fell off the only toilet in the trailer. Champ's mother and I had to spend the night at a motel in town and try to find someone to fix it. Emil Friedrich, a friend of ours, came out early the next morning and put in a new commode. He did mention that some of the pipes had frozen so we had to rig the sink/shower with a hose from the back yard. It didn't look very nice sticking through the window, but it was better than having no water at all. Cooking was a bit more complicated without the use of water in the sink, but we managed to get the food prepared just in time for the company's arrival. We visited while the last minute details were tended to and then we filled our plates and went outside to the picnic tables for the meal. The 45- degree temperature turned the hot food to cold in less than two minutes. The gravy was icy. Everyone went back inside and ate with their meals in their laps.

Matt's First Buck

Matthew (age nine) killed his first buck at this lease and I was sitting with him when he shot it. He had missed one the day before and was most unhappy about it soooo after Thanksgiving lunch, while the Dallas Cowboys were on television and most of the men were either glued to the game or snoring in their chairs, we headed off to the nearest deer blind. It was a rather grey day, misting and windy. The men warned us several times that we wouldn't see anything at that time of day and that we were just wasting our time. It was about 2:00 p.m. when the handsome six-point buck stepped out of the brush and calmly walked over to the feeder. Matthew saw him first and nudged me to get out of his way. He had to open the window on the north side of the blind to get his gun in the proper position to shoot. Of course, it made a loud squeaking noise as he slowly tried to open it. The deer looked around but didn't run away. Matthew aimed at the deer and squeezed the trigger but the bullet sailed right over the middle of the buck's back. He pulled the gun back into the blind, got a shell out of his pocket and re-loaded. All the while I was experiencing buck fever. My hands were sweaty and my throat, dry. I kept encouraging him to hurry, but the more I said, the longer it seemed to take. Finally, he aimed a second time and fired the gun. The deer fell. Matthew and I leaped out of the blind and rushed over to see it. Matthew didn't have enough shells left in his pocket to fire the signal of a downed deer (three quick shots) so he decided to run back to the camp and ask for help. As he was leaving, he handed me his knife and said, "Mom, if he tries to get up, slit his throat!"

Driving and Crashing

The boys learned to drive at the Hill Country ranch - out of harm's way - or so we thought. It seemed the perfect place to let them take the wheel and learn the first few things about driving trucks, trail bikes, tractors, and such. Well, it seemed that way in the beginning.

Michael enjoyed driving the tractor until the nose reared up on him and he nearly fell off of it. He particularly enjoyed riding the trail bike until he drove it smack into the side of our mobile home. Matthew wrapped the pickup around a telephone pole on one occasion, and rammed the trail bike into the picnic table while Champ and I were sitting on it another time. Mitchell couldn't manage the stick shift in the small truck very well and accidentally (maybe or maybe not) threw Michael out of the back. Rich Hull, a young friend from Dallas, turned the trail bike over somewhere in the brush and then couldn't find it. There was never a dull moment.

Perhaps the best recalled and most retold story was about the day Matthew shot Old Yeller (the truck). He and Michael were driving off to do a little hunting and Mike asked Matt if his gun was loaded. Matt said he thought it was, but would look just to be sure. He opened the chamber and saw a shell. When he snapped the gun back together, the gun went off, and blew a hole in the floor board. Mike didn't know just where the bullet landed and yelled for Matthew to get out quickly before the truck exploded. They both jumped out as fast as they could and Michael ran back to the camp to tell us all about it. (We had heard the shot and were afraid something had gone wrong because they had not been gone long enough to get to the closest blind.) Mike was so animated, he couldn't get the words out fast enough. Matthew, on the other hand, was not so quick to tell the story. We didn't see hide nor hair of him for quite some time. When he did return (rather sheepishly), he apologized for killing the truck. Actually it didn't hurt anything but the floor board and Matthew's pride. But from then on, the hole in the floor was a good conversation starter for anyone who sat on the passenger's side of the front seat of the pickup.

Opening Day

Michael has always been our most avid deer hunter and has always been willing to spend lots of time preparing for the hunt. One year he was determined to be in the deer blind before first light on the first day of the season to get his chance at "Butch". The night before, he laid out all the gear he needed and checked it over a couple of times to be sure he had everything he might possible want: long johns; jeans; a camouflage shirt; a couple pairs of socks; warm boots; parka-style jacket; a knitted cap with small holes for the eyes and nose; warm gloves with the trigger finger missing; binoculars; a sharp knife; a canteen for hot chocolate; and the deer rifle and shells. He was all set and went to bed earlier than usual.

He wasn't in the blind more than a few minutes before he saw a 10 or 11 point buck come out of the brush but, before he could take aim, another good buck stepped out. The two deer clashed antlers several times and, in the dim light, Mike couldn't get a good shot at either one of them. He waited a few seconds and then fired. He wasn't sure if either one had been hit, but he got out of the blind and rushed over to see. Actually, both bucks were on the ground.

It wasn't far from the ground to the skillet. The Hill Country venison tasted quite a bit different from that of the deer in South Texas, mainly due to the difference in the vegetation of that area. There was no strong odor while the meat was cooking and there was no need to marinate the meat to tenderize it. In fact, if you processed your deer meat with some of the local German sausage, the finished product was good enough to serve at parties and other special occasions. Doe harvesting wasn't quite so distasteful (ha! ha!) as one might have expected and we encouraged our guests to do their part.

We often had friends and relatives come to the deer lease for a visit. Most of the young people were happy to get the chance to hunt and thrilled at the prospect of shooting a doe. Michael was always patient with beginners and was willing to sit with guests in the deer blind, to give them tips on what to do and what not to do, and to show them how to clean the deer if they shot one. Several cousins learned how to "field dress" a deer right in our back yard. Of course boys and girls alike had to have their shirt tails cut when they killed their first deer - a hunting tradition.

The Campfire

Building a barbeque pit right out in the front of the mobile home was a top priority when we first bought the ranch. Champ took great pride in designing it and seeing that the boys actually built it. There were plenty of rocks around in the yard and it didn't take our sons long to put it together with a little cement. It was not only a barbeque pit; it was the campfire setting. Most evenings we would sit out around it, have a few drinks, roast a little meat for dinner, and tell amusing stories or events of the day. It was most enjoyable (unless you happened to get your boots too close to the fire or the meat fell into the coals or the bats darted around your head or the "cool of the evening" became the "cold of the night"). Our neighbors couldn't quite understand why we would prefer to sit out around the fire when we had a perfectly warm trailer just a few feet away. Obviously, they hadn't been exposed to the hunting traditions of deep South Texas.

The Ticks

No matter how nice it was to walk among the cedars or how pleasant it was to stroll through the meadows, if you found ticks on your clothes and on your person (even worse), you were in for an unfortunate experience. Ticks tended to migrate to the warmest body spots and bury themselves there. Home remedies for removing them ranged from covering the ticks with lanolin or fingernail polish to burning them out with a cigarette lighter. None ever worked well for my boys. Usually a day or two of miserable itching was the final result.

The Turkey Shoot (Or Not)

One day, Champ devised a plan to hunt turkey just east of the main entrance road and bought some camouflage netting to disguise the ground blind close to the pond. Beto Villegas and Matthew had already strategically positioned themselves on either side of the anticipated route the turkey would take and lay there very quietly. Champ set up a couple of chairs, picked up his binoculars and his brand new turkey caller, and took me to the blind.

I really didn't like the sound of the turkey caller. It had a rasping sound with a rather high pitch, and I was sure no intelligent tom turkey was ever going to be fooled by it. My husband, on the other hand, was positive it would work if we just gave it enough time. He called and I shuddered; he called and I shuddered. He called, and a huge gobbler ran right down the road toward us. I got so excited, I hopped up out of my seat and hollered, "There he is!" By the time any of the hunters could take aim, the turkey had turned tail and flown the coop. Poor guys!

The Hurricane Turned Tornado

Hurricane Allen was heading for the Valley area back in the summer of 1980. Our family had boarded up the windows and stored up water and groceries so we could wait out the storm at home. Most of our friends had decided to head either north to San Antonio or west to Laredo to avoid the storm's wrath.

Early the day the storm was supposed to hit the coast, Champ was listening to the weather station in Brownsville and the announcer was truly alarmed. After giving his report about the intensity of the storm and its imminent danger, he said, "And may God help us all." Those words caused Champ to change his mind about staying home. We gathered our children, a few clothes, and Champ's mom, and headed north. There wasn't enough room in the station wagon for Goldie, our retriever, to go along and the boys were all crying when we had to leave her behind.

The rains had already begun to come in waves and we knew we were on the outer edge of the storm. The highways were mostly deserted; only a single car or truck came by now and then. It was eerie! We drove with our ears tuned to the radio, but lost the signal before we got to Alice. Every little town was boarded up, with only a few people venturing out. It was like being in a science fiction film.

After several hours of traveling, we stopped for lunch at a restaurant north of San Antonio and called Champ's brother, Guy, in McAllen, to see what had happened at home. He reported that the storm had gone in north of Port Mansfield and was no longer a threat to our area. What a relief! We all relaxed and enjoyed the lunch and rode on to the ranch to spend the night.

We didn't realize the storm was headed our way until we unloaded the car and settled into camp. The newscast was disheartening. There was talk about tornados in the local area, downed power lines and loss of electricity. The winds raged and the lightning lit up the sky. We had traveled 300 miles to avoid the storm, but it caught up with us in Central Texas.

Highways 77 and 281 were closed for most of the next week but we took the western route through Laredo to get home. So did everyone else trying to get back to check out any damage done to their personal property. The traffic was awful and the kids were restless. They were impatient to see what had happened to their beloved pet. When we finally arrived in Donna, we found Goldie alive and well, and mighty pleased to see us.

She had weathered the storm far better than we had.

The Big Ranch Deer Lease

Talk about taking a step up! Wow! From the first time we set foot on this lease until the last day we were there, every trip was filled with new and exciting adventures. You could write a book about the eleven years we were fortunate enough to hunt a few miles north of Raymondville, but that would take ages. I hope to give you just a few of the highlights.

While we were in the process of deciding whether or not we wanted to hunt on this lease, we took a ride around a small portion of the 20,000 acres. It was incredible to see the large number of bucks running together (often as many as 10 or 15) and the huge flocks of turkeys (60 or more birds). There were herds of javelina and unlimited numbers of quail coveys. It took your breath away!

Because they had not been hunted, the game didn't run away when someone approached them. The bucks often didn't get up from their resting places, but looked at people with as much curiosity as people looked at them. There was a particular three-mile stretch of road which was nicknamed "Buck Alley", because one rarely rode through that area without seeing at least one buck. We saw at least six or seven good bucks the very first time we drove through it. The decision was not "if" we wanted to be on this lease; it was "how soon" could we pay to get on this lease.

We pulled our two little travel trailers out to our chosen spot, poured a little concrete for a patio, and were in the hunting business. The boys were thrilled with every bit of this new lease and had great ideas about where they wanted to set up their blinds. Each son had to look at several sites before he could make a decision and, of course, we had to know where the other 15 families were going to put their blinds.(One would think that with 20,000 acres to choose from, there wouldn't be much competition for a single spot, but one would be wrong.) After much conferring, deer blinds and feeders were put in place and the hunting began in earnest. What fun to see all the game! But, as the ranch cowboys told us, you could see a lot more if you hunted from your pickup. No need to sit in a blind where your opportunities were limited; you could hunt countless acres soooo we learned to hunt from the truck.

It may sound as though the deer didn't have a chance, but Mother Nature protects her own. I can remember on one occasion, the older boys were encouraging Mitchell to shoot a buck they had seen the day before. We drove to the area and spotted the big buck lying in the shade under a mesquite tree. Champ turned on the four-wheel drive and headed right across the field toward him. He didn't move. We got within 20 yards of him and he didn't seem to care. Well, Mitchell was not going to shoot a deer while it was napping! The boys hollered at the deer and waved their hands all around and, finally, it managed to get to its feet and walk away. Guess it was not overly intimidated by our presence. We waited a few minutes to give it a fair chance at sur-

Bucks at the Camp Feeder.

vival, and it walked into a copse of trees and was gone. We drove up and down the senderos on either side of the tree line, but we never saw him again. His legs looked just like the tree branches and he became invisible. Moral: one deer on the ground is better than one in the bush! Ha. Ha. Just kidding.

Large Indian antelopes lived on the Big Ranch and the very first time Matthew saw a nilgai doe, he was incredulous. He pointed her out and exclaimed that he had just seen the biggest doe of his life. However, it was obvious she was not a white-tail deer by the manner in which she turned and loped away. We often saw the nilgai bulls, but they were quite skittish and didn't stick around long. They were huge animals, often weighing as much as 750 pounds, with shorter hind legs than front legs, and with thick, stinky hides. Rolling in the dirt was bathing to them and you can imagine their odor, but their meat was delicious. Our family preferred it to beef.

You had to think twice before you shot a nilgai. It was difficult enough to get a field-dressed animal into the back of a pickup (due to its sheer weight), but if you shot one on the other side of a fence, you really had your work cut out for you.

Michael killed several nilgai during our years on the lease, but once when I was along on an early morning ride, he shot a bull and it took four of us to push/pull/tug it into the bed of the pickup. Fortunately, it only weighed about 350 pounds. Another time, when we were quail hunting, we turned into a rather secluded area and saw a nilgai doe nursing her fawn. I'll never forget that sight.

Egrets were everywhere and geese often landed on the ponds and lakes. Waterfowl were fun to watch and we spent many an early morning or late afternoon sitting by the pond. Several of the hunters put up duck blinds, but I don't remember our having much luck in that area. Almost all of the game eventually came to the pond for a drink before nightfall and during the driest part of the summer, you could often see animals which would normally avoid one another come at the same time. The most interesting birds we saw were six whooping cranes. At one point not too many years ago, they were on the brink of extinction, and it was wonderful to see them in the wild. Another time there were so many

Thank Heaven for Laughter

geese huddled together at the north end of the lease, they gave the appearance of being a rather large lake. What a surprise it was to see them rise into the air!

Turkey flocks often had fifty or more birds. They gobbled and they called, and they made their way through the thickest of brush with the greatest of ease. We had wild turkey for a meal only once. Enough said!

Snakes were king-sized. Six-foot rattlers were not uncommon and were found fairly often. The only good thing about their size was the ability to spot one from a distance. Our grandson saw one from the truck about 25 feet away. That was close enough for his dad to jump out and shoot it, but far enough to be out of harm's way. Neighbors had several snake-in-the-camp stories to tell, but we didn't have any that I know about.

We did have a couple of snake stories from the past, though. Michael had his first experience at the Salinas Ranch. He was walking along with some of the other hunters and spied a rattler several feet away, under some brush. He yelled out, "Rattler!", jumped three feet into the air, made a 180-degree turn, and was gone before any of the others could even react. His lightning-quick reflexes were a true asset that day. Another time Matthew killed a rattler crossing the road and took it home to show his friends. He stretched the skin out on a board and put it up on the roof to let the sun dry it out. After a couple of weeks, it was cured. He asked me to make it into a hatband for him, and I had to iron the skin to smooth it out. Oh, the stench! It was really ghastly! (What mothers do for their children!!!) I sewed the skin together at the back of his hat and added the rattles as well. Matthew wore that hat proudly for a couple of weeks before the dog got hold of it and tore the hatband to shreds.

We did have a skunk living under the cook shack and I did get to see him up close and personal. One of the bird dogs got wind of the critter and crawled under the building, trying to corner the skunk. The dog's tail kept hitting the underside of the kitchen floor as he barked and growled, and then the dog's tail began to hit the floor less and less often. He seemed to be stuck. Matthew worried that the high-strung dog was going to kill itself in its determination to get to the skunk so he went out with his shovel to dig the dog out. When he shined the light at the skunk, it decided to make a run for it. It ran past Matt and right toward me. I was sitting on the porch watching all the excitement when the skunk darted in my direction. It was covered with dirt and I wasn't sure what it was until it went by. Then there was no doubt. Fortunately, it didn't spray me but the cook shack never smelled the same again! The dog did survive the ordeal, but it didn't do any hunting for the next few days.

Quail coveys were around every turn in the road, down every sendero. There was no lack of quail. We didn't hunt with bird dogs, but never failed to get our share of birds. One morning Champ and two of the boys got their limits in less than 45 minutes. It was fun for the boys to spend time together with their dad and to bring home the birds for me to cook. I enjoyed their having so much fun (and their plucking the birds), I didn't mind frying the quail. It is still one of their all-time favorite meals. (For those of you who don't know, quail have a very short life span, and if we don't eat them, coyotes, road-runners, or hawks will.)

After a couple of years on the lease, we got rid of the mouse-ridden trailer and, at Matthew's insistence, brought in a metal building we remodeled into a house. It was about 60 feet long and had a master bedroom, a bathroom (tub and all), and a large sleeping area which could accommodate six to eight people. It was super to have the bath tub. In the midst of all the sand and dirt, there was still a place one could have a bubble bath and I did on many an occasion. The grandchildren also loved to spend time in the tub with their toys.

It was beginning to be our "home away from home" and we spent at least one night every weekend on the ranch. If we spent Saturday night, I could always get up early and be home in time for Sunday School and church because it was just about an hour's drive from Donna.

The rules the Big Ranch management made for each lessee were lenient enough. Although you had to be present, it didn't make any difference if you shot the game yourself or if your friends shot the game. You were responsible for what was killed and you were ac-

Thank Heaven for Laughter

countable for recording it. It did enable us to take our friends and our sons' friends and that made it all the more enjoyable for everyone. We were particularly happy to take our friends from England (The Swallows) on a camera tour and they were so impressed with the game they saw, they asked to bring other friends of theirs to see it as well. Friends and relatives all looked forward to having a weekend at the deer lease.

One of Matt's college friends, Lance Kirby, came to visit us during the Christmas holidays one year and enjoyed hunting with us on the Big Ranch lease. He was amazed at the amount of game we saw, but even more amazed at what the boys would and would not consider shooting.

Every time they had a buck in their sight, they discussed its Boone & Crockett qualifications before taking aim. They often passed up very nice deer because the rack was not exceptional - either not wide enough, or high enough, or non-symmetrical, or lacking dropped tines, or something! It was most frustrating for those of us just watching. Several days of finding, but not reaping were difficult to believe. Most hunters would have been delighted with any of the game we chose not to shoot.

After he left the Valley, Lance sent me a thank-you note on stationery that had a very large buck with a very large rack in the upper right-hand corner. His question was, "Is this one a shooter?" Ha! Ha!

Each of the boys killed several nice bucks and had the racks mounted while we were hunting on this lease, but the biggest trophy belonged to our daughter-in-law, Kelli Jones. She usually preferred reading to hunting while we were at the lease, but she was in the right place at the right time and shot a big 10 pointer with an impressive rack.

You didn't really have to leave the campsite to enjoy the animals. Every campsite had its own feeder and the deer and feral hogs would travel from one site to another on a regular basis. We became so familiar with the animals, we knicknamed some of the deer that came around most often. The deer were so tame that you could actually sit and have dinner on the patio 15 feet from them and they never moved away. They became so accustomed to having people around, they didn't even mind the children's noisy toys or their crying. Corn was uppermost on their minds.

One spring morning, we had four tom turkeys strut through our camp with their tail feathers fanned out, obviously trying to get the attention of some hens in the next yard. The girls didn't even look up. The gobblers strode back and forth for quite some time and even allowed us to step out and take their pictures. They impressed us, but they didn't impress the hens.

I must mention the vehicles hunters used. Our rig was just a Chevy four-wheel drive pickup with a quail rack on the bed, which raised the hunters up in the air about five feet.

It was amazing how much more you could see from that vantage point than you could from the inside of the cab. Often someone would signal that he could see some game from the top and the driver couldn't see anything at all. Of course, it was the brush that got in the way. It was bumpy up there and colder than being on the inside, but children and adults alike preferred to be on top most of the time. Even my aunt and uncle wanted to take a turn up there just last year and they were in their 70's.

Three Boys, Two Dogs and a Dead Deer.

You wouldn't believe how elaborate some of the other hunting vehicles were. Many of them were camouflage-painted jeeps or trucks with features especially designed for the avid hunter. One man had a two-level vehicle which could be driven from about 15 feet in the air. These folks were serious about their deer hunting.

It was truly a sad day in March when we were asked to leave the Big Ranch lease. There had been a change in management and all hunters were told to remove their camping facilities and be gone within three months' time. We were stunned by the news. Some of the other hunters were angry, but I was so happy to have had 11 wonderful years there, I couldn't be.

Los Encinitos near Rachel

It didn't take Champ long to find another lease. Some of the other hunters moved to a 20,000 acre ranch just west of Rachel, and Champ needed little coaxing to join them. The campsite had to be carved out of a copse of oak trees and electricity had to be brought to the site, but the hunters were ready for the new season long before November.

We had sold our old buildings to a fellow hunter and had to find new accommodations for this lease. What a delightful surprise was in store for me! Champ bought a used mobile home for a reasonable price that had three bedrooms, two baths, AND a washer-dryer. It might as well have been the "Taj Mahal." We could sleep all our children and their children quite comfortably and we didn't have to lug the laundry back and forth to Donna. Hurrah! Hurrah!

The deer on this lease were not so plentiful, but there were enough big bucks to challenge an experienced hunter. Quail abounded. Coveys and coveys of them could be seen and/or heard as you drove down the roads. Some had as many as 20 birds or more.

Turkey were constantly in the campsite, and the grandchildren were always happy to see them strut through the yard. Snakes were everywhere! Several were killed right behind the mobile home and we had to take great measures to guard against them. One day last year we spotted a fairly large mountain lion, but couldn't get close enough to get his picture. We did, however, try to find his tracks in the sand, but couldn't make them out. You never know what's around the bend or down the next road when you go hunting. As Michael often says, " That's why it's called hunting and not finding."

Our oldest grandson, Clay, killed his first buck here just a week or so before his ninth birthday and our oldest granddaughter, Chelsea, killed her first buck here just one week later. Their father, Michael, was instrumental in finding the deer, but they did the shooting.

What great times our family has shared at all of the different leases! (Champ, Matthew and his family are there as I write these words and it's 100 degrees outside in late June. Our youngest grandsons, Forrest and Joshua, always dress for the occasion, no matter the temperature. They wear boots, camouflage outfits, and coonskin caps. Even Emily, their baby sister, wears ruffled camouflage bloomers!)

Thanksgiving at the Ranch 2003.

Trout Fishing in the Channel

In 1990 the law firm bought a pier in the channel and a 20-foot in-board/out-board boat went along with the purchase. We were anxious to try fishing under the lights and decided to take some friends along to enjoy the adventure with us. Champ made a list of all the items we would need to spend our first night there and it was rather lengthy: a generator, cooking utensils, breakfast foods, pillows, candles, matches, tools, fishing gear, measuring tape, etc.

Jimmie and Barbara Steidinger, his cousin (Pete Braun), Champ, Mitchell and I drove to the arroyo and piled into the boat loaded down with all the supplies. We headed east toward the channel and found ourselves almost to the point of capsizing. Other boats made waves which nearly swamped ours so we had to travel at a very slow pace. What should have taken 30 minutes, took nearly two hours. A Coast Guard boat came by and hailed us but then backed off, afraid of drowning us. It was getting dark when we reached the pier and we barely had enough time to get the generator going before the sun disappeared.

To my surprise there were no beds! There were only long narrow benches to sleep on and the only bathroom facility was a joke! It was an open-air affair with three sides and a hole in the seat. I am sure menfolk considered it to be sufficient for their needs, but it was lacking in several departments as far as I was concerned. Fortunately, the whirring noise of the generator muffled any sound coming from that area. The tell-tale tissue floating in the water was plenty embarrassing but couldn't be disguised.

We cooked dinner and settled in for a night of fantastic fishing. And we were not disappointed! Fish literally jumped on the lines. We caught two at a time until our arms couldn't cast any more. It was unbelievable! It didn't seem to matter which lure you used, the fish liked them all. I had bruises on my waist from the sheer weight of the rod digging into my flesh, and I just kept right on fishing. A barge came by and that deterred the fish for an hour or so, but then they were back and biting each time we cast once more. It was a fisherman's dream come true.

About midnight we tried to get some sleep, but that wasn't as easy as the fishing had been. It was extremely difficult to straddle the bench. It was a very long time before the sun came up and when it did, we realized that the fish basket had turned over and only a few fish were still in it. (I know this sounds like a typical fish story, but this one is true.)

It was hot and humid on the water and we were quick to start back to the arroyo. Due to the lightened load, we were home in short order.

Several weeks later, we decided to have another go at the pier. Some of the planks on the dock had rotted out, and Jimmie was going to replace them. This time we arrived well before dark and actually accomplished quite a bit of repair work. Unfortunately, Champ tried to push the boat away from a nail at the end of the pier with his foot and fell into the water. He careened off the side of the boat and bruised his rib-cage. He was in great pain, but didn't want to go back to town.

The sun went down, we ate dinner, and we fished. It was great fun for the Steidingers and me, but Champ couldn't find any place to get comfortable, not sitting on the bench, not lying on the bench, not anywhere. Finally, we decided to strap him to the seat at the front of the boat. (I know that sounds cruel, but it was the only way he could sit erect, ease the pain in his side, and not fall into the water if he fell asleep.) Well, of course, it was a serious situation, but one couldn't help chuckling just a bit. It's not every day you tie a fellow to his boat. Champ remained outside floating on the boat, moaning and groaning between snores, until the first rays of morning appeared. (You just have to smile at that thought!) Then we were off toward home and the doctor's office. Although his ribs had been separated, no bones were broken and only one ego was bruised.

Bass Fishing in Mexico

Bass fishing in northern Mexico was/is one of our family's favorite sports. As soon as the older boys were big enough (8 and 5), Champ planned a long weekend of fishing for us at the Lago Vista Fishing Lodge located on Lake Guerrero. The 200-mile drive was accomplished in just three hours; the planning and packing took three days.

The camp itself was fairly new and had all the modern conveniences. The swimming pool had not yet been completed, but I wasn't too disappointed. I could just as easily read a book or something while the guys went fishing. I was simply going to relax and enjoy the place - no cooking, no cleaning, no schedules to meet.

Champ intended to fish twice each day so he hired a guide and a boat well in advance of our trip. The first day of fishing went according to plan and all three boys had great fun out on the lake. The second night there was a different story. Champ and I had a drink in the bar after dinner, and Champ didn't come out, at least not until way late in the evening. I tried to coerce him into coming back to our room on a couple of occasions, but he had met some fellow hunters whose plane had crash-landed several hours earlier that evening, and he wanted to hear their stories. Finally, it became obvious that we were having a contest of wills and I had absolutely no chance of winning, so I gave up and went to bed. I heard him come though the door sometime after midnight, and then we all heard him snore the rest of the night. When the guide tapped on the door at 5:00 a.m., signaling it was time to have breakfast, Champ didn't feel up to the trip. I ranted and raved and scolded him for behaving poorly and for depriving the boys of their last chance to fish. I admonished him for spending so much money for the boat and then not being able to use it. He quietly suggested I take them myself.

Was this a dare? It sounded like a dare to me. The little boys were anxious to go soooo what could I say in response? Yes, I would take them myself! We dressed quickly and went to breakfast. There were 25 men in the dining room, two little boys and me that Sunday morning. (You talk about a fish out of water. Ha! Ha!) Any uncomfortable feelings I might have had were dispelled when the men sang a few hymns before they left for their boats. I wasn't expecting a Christian worship service in this out-of-the-way place, but it was a most pleasant surprise.

The boys and I followed the guide to the boat and got in. I could tell we were going to have a communication problem from the outset. My Spanish vocabulary centered around household activities and his English was non-existent. We had to rely on hand motions to get our ideas across. Wow! One minute on the boat and we were up to about 30 miles an hour, darting around trees and tree trunks in the water. We flew by them with precious little room to spare (inches on either side). My heart was pounding. I wondered if we were going to survive! The boys, on the other hand, were enjoying every minute of the fast-paced ride. Thirty minutes went by before our guide decided to stop and fish. He helped the boys with their fishing rods, and I just sat back and offered a few prayers of thanksgiving. We caught nothing. The sun was up and the temperature was rising. We caught nothing some more. The guide pulled up the anchor after an hour or so, and we moved (quickly) to another spot on the lake. I was beginning to wish I hadn't had that cup of coffee for breakfast. There were no facilities anywhere I could see and the pressure was getting to be most uncomfortable. I tried to make my concerns known to the young guide but he didn't comprehend. At last I asked Michael to make some gestures that would get the message across. Immediately, the young man pulled up the anchor and away we went across the lake. I was counting the minutes it might take to get back to the camp but I was in for another surprise. We stopped at a very small island. Not a tree or a bush could be seen! We had passed several boats on our way there, but none were visible at the moment soooo I made for shore. Of course, the guys had to look the other direction, and my boys made sure the guide did, too.

I was certain the guide would take us back to the camp at this late hour (10:00 a.m.) but, no, we were going to get our whole morning's fishing - whether we wanted it or not!

After another hour or so of not catching anything, we headed in. The ride back was just as fast-paced and dangerous as the earlier one, but at least we were going in the right direction.

Champ was feeling better by the time we got back to the room. We were all happy for him.

Parasailing at Padre - 1984

Our 25th high school class reunion was an occasion to remember. We wanted to do something special so we planned to hold the event at South Padre Island, Texas. About 75 people showed up for the affair, including classmates, spouses and a few significant others. We enjoyed a wonderful buffet by the pool and took advantage of the ocean view.

It was a fantastic setting in which to reminisce about the "good old days" of the late fifties. How wonderful to see how little some of us had changed and how good life had been to most of us. Getting to know about each others' children and spouses was interesting and many classmates brought family photos to share.

After all the group activities were over the first evening, several of the girls got together for a talkathon which ended well into the wee hours. We talked about old times, getting married, having babies (all the girly stuff), and then we began talking about exciting events we had done or wished we had done. One thing led to another and pretty soon we were debating whether or not some of us should dare to go parasailing the next day. After all, here we were in our 40's and if we didn't do it now, when would we ever have the nerve? One girl said she would definitely go, another said she would if I did, and soooo I agreed to give it a try. We planned to be ready to go early the next morning before any of us could back out!

It still seemed like a good idea the next morning when I got up and put my bathing suit on under my shorts (just on the odd chance I fell into the water). The three of us were on the boat just after 9:00

a.m. The sun was shining brightly, the sea was rather calm, and the breeze was not too gusty - all the weather conditions were conducive for parasailing.

It was with a little trepidation that I stepped onto the boat, knowing there was no opportunity for escape at this late date. Elizabeth Dalton was good enough to say she would take the first turn and I quickly thanked God that I didn't have to lead the way. She got into the basket seat, put on the harness, and smiled as the young boat captain told her what to expect. He began to unwind the cable, allowing her to slowly rise up and away from the boat. She never actually disappeared from sight, but she did get way up in the air. (I was getting a bit anxious at this point). We headed north along the row of condos and hotels for about five minutes and then made a wide turn and headed back. Her turn seemed to last a short time, but then... I had to prepare myself (and my heart) for my turn. My hands were sweaty and my heart was beating ever so fast!

The basket seat was small and I just barely fit into it. The harness was a means of security, but it wasn't nearly strong enough to make me feel comfortable. I gripped the rope as tightly as I could and faintly smiled as he reeled me up into the air. The boat seemed fairly large at first; then it got smaller and smaller until it seemed like a small dot way down below me. The rope rubbed grudgingly against the metal basket and made an eerie noise, as though at any minute the rope might break. A small private plane flew by and I could see the passengers inside. One of them actually waved at me, but I was too scared to take my hands off the harness to return the friendly gesture. (I was holding on so tightly, my knuckles were actually white.) I was sailing as high as some of the top floors of the beachfront hotels and condos and could actually see in their windows. No one was up there with me, except God, of course. Need I say that a few more prayers were offered up during this ride?

After what seemed an eternity, the boat made the wide turn and we started back toward our hotel. What a difference that made! Now, I was really beginning to enjoy blowing in the wind. The rocking back and forth wasn't so bad after all and the noise of the rubbing rope wasn't as scary as it had first seemed. As we neared the hotel, some of our classmates came out to cheer us on, and I actually managed to take one hand off the harness and wave to them. The descent was the best part of the trip! The boat grew larger and larger and, before I knew it, I was safely back on board. The whole trip had taken less than 10 minutes.

Annie Dahl took her turn while Elizabeth and I shared our thoughts about the experience. It seemed only a few minutes before we were back on shore with our friends, urging all of them to sign up for a ride. I don't remember if any one did, but it was another experience of a lifetime for me.

Rafting on the River

I am sure many of you have had the pleasure of floating down a river on a raft, but the morning I took some very good friends from England and some very good family members on a trip down the Guadalupe River near New Braunfels, Texas, is one that none of us will ever forget.

I invited Helga Swallow, her 17-year old twins (boy, Chris, and girl, Nicky), one of their friends from Britain, my sister Eloise and her daughter, Gigi, to spend a few hours rafting. We had taken a boat ride on the San Antonio River the night before and everyone really enjoyed it so off we went. None of us was properly dressed for the event. We had on shorts, sandals, and dresses, no bathing suits or swimming gear. We rented a raft for eight, took a short bus ride upstream, received a few words of advice and a small map and life jackets enough for everyone, and proceeded to put the boat in the water. In less than two minutes, we were in desperate trouble! Instead of heading right down the river, we each started rowing in a different direction, hit a large boulder and Nicky fell into the water. Helga was horrified! Chris thought it was funny! As we struggled to get her back into the raft, we were thrown up against more rocks jutting out of the water. At one point, we got off the regular route and ended up in water too shallow to float. We had to get out and wade about 200 yards over slippery rocks (wearing sandals, no less) while Chris carried the raft down to deeper water. It was particularly difficult for Eloise who had bad knees and Gigi had to guide her slowly through the rocky terrain. All this took place in less than 30 minutes and we had several more miles of river to travel.

College kids on inner tubes (drinking beer and listening to loud music) passed us by and laughed. A man in a kayak going upstream saw us in distress, smiled in our direction, and just kept going. Even the turtles sunning themselves on the bank seemed to be amused by our dilemma. No one offered to help us.

There were a few lulls in the action. Part of the time we actually floated down the river and had time to notice the beautiful trees hanging out over the water. We enjoyed watching the turtles bask in the warm sunshine and seeing the sun's rays shimmer on the water. However, before long, we could hear the rapids ahead of us and someone would shout out, "White water!!!!", and we would all promise to row in the same direction. It just didn't happen! Every time there was a boulder in the middle of the river, we seemed to aim for it, not around it. Poor Chris had six women to help him navigate the rapids and we failed him miserably.

After three long, very long hours (180 minutes), we could see the low-water bridge where we were to end the trip. Prayers of thanks were lifted by one and all. Still, we had one more obstacle to overcome. The river was moving quite rapidly at this point and if

Rafting on the Guadalupe.

we didn't make a sharp turn just in front of the bridge, we could all have been decapitated. Believe it or not, this one time we all rowed in the same direction!!!

Happy to be on shore and happy to be alive, we calmly got in our cars and started home. No one spoke for quite some time, and then we didn't stop talking about it for the next 250 miles. Everyone had been on the same raft, but each one of us had a different experience and a different story to tell.

Snowmobiling - 1993

My niece, Gigi, and Rob Stinson were planning to be married in Lake Tahoe the first part of March. It was going to be a small affair, with only three or four couples of their close friends attending. Eloise and Rob's mother, Doris Fullington, wanted desperately to be there, too, soooo they invited me to go along and surprise the bride and groom.

The plane trip was a riotous ride. We laughed all the way; telling jokes and imagining how the kids would react when we walked into the ceremony at the last minute. It was fun listening to stories about Rob's childhood and telling amusing stories about Gigi's growing-up years. We giggled and we laughed. Most, not all, of the passengers in the neighboring rows were laughing with us. What fun!

It was late when we arrived at our hotel so we went to bed early, and didn't have to avoid being seen by Gigi and Rob. However, we had just ordered breakfast the next morning when they suddenly appeared at our table. Gigi had spotted us and was in disbelief. She asked Rob if those ladies didn't look like people he knew and he had to agree that we looked very familiar.

Gigi and one of her friends, Becky Weich, were planning to spend part of the day snowmobiling and invited us to go. Eloise declined, but Doris thought it would be a great idea soooo we agreed to join them. The trip to the gear shop was a brand new experience for me. I didn't realize we would have to wear special shoes, gloves and head gear. Sun glasses were a must, too. When I finally came out of the shop, I looked and felt like I weighed 200 lbs.

Doris had often ridden on the back of a bike so she insisted that I drive the snow mobile. What? I had never driven any kind of motor bike and didn't think this was the time to learn, but she assured me I would be fine at the wheel. The bike was much heavier than I expected, and I was more than a little antsy. It seemed prudent to at least let the tour leader know how much of a novice I was, and he agreed we should be okay if I just followed directly behind him. That sounded easy enough. He instructed us on the basic parts of the bike (I didn't even know how to start it), and gave us all a few words of warning about not wandering off the beaten path. The snow drifts were quite deep and people could easily get into trouble if they didn't carefully watch where they were going. He got my attention.

We started off at about 25 miles per hour, with Gigi and Becky following close behind. They laughed and joked at every bump in the road, but I was seriously concerned about living through this adventure. I didn't take my eyes off of the ruts in the road ahead of us. Occasionally I could hear the others exclaiming over the fantastic beauty of the area, but still I didn't dare look away. To add to the dilemma, the steering wheel warmer was working overtime and I didn't know how to turn it off. I could barely keep my hands on the wheel, it was so hot. Over the mountain and through the woods we went. We rode for almost an hour before we stopped for a break and an opportunity to take photos. If I could have walked back to the starting point, I would have gladly done so. The tour leader was kind enough to turn off the warmer so the return ride was not so uncomfortable for me, but I still kept my eyes on the center of the road.

What a delightful feeling to get out of all that gear. I felt like a new person. I had seen all the snow I wanted to see right on the ground in front of me. There wasn't enough time for a nap before the wedding, so I settled for a hot bubble bath. It was there that I began to think back over the day's activities and began to smile.

Gigi and Rob were married in a chapel overlooking Lake Tahoe that afternoon and are now living happily ever after.

Hot Air Ballooning

Once again we were off on an excursion with Charles and Flo Kennedy. This time we headed for Canada and spent several days in and around Banff. The scenery was breath-taking, especially the view of Lake Louise with the snow-capped mountains in the background. The turquoise shade of the water was indescribable; it didn't look real. It looked as though someone had painted it.

We took a sight-seeing train, The Rocky Mountaineer, from Calgary to Vancouver, and what a trip that was! There were three-course meals served for breakfast and lunch and snacks in between; there were huge windows for panoramic viewing of the scenery; and there were great recliner seats large enough to accommodate most every size and shape.

The first day of the journey was almost 12 hours long, but there was much to see and, of course, there was a guide telling us the history of the area and amusing stories so we had no time to be bored (and little time to sleep). We saw a black bear scurrying away from the track; we saw osprey nests built on top of abandoned telephone poles; we saw Indians fishing in the rivers with nets; and we saw plenty of snow and lots of mountains.

We didn't end our trip in Vancouver; we continued on to Victoria Island by ferry. It was late in the evening when we finally arrived at our bed-and-breakfast. Some of our luggage had been "temporarily misplaced" so we had to buy toothbrushes and other toiletries in case we had to do without some of our personal items overnight. The accommodations were very nice, but our room was on the third floor of the house. The winding staircase was small and it was quite a challenge to climb at the end of a long day. No sooner had we settled in and gotten comfortable than the desk clerk rang to say that our luggage had been delivered by taxi and we could come down and get it at our convenience. He would be glad to help, but there was no one to watch the front desk so he couldn't possibly leave his post. There was nothing to do but traipse down the stairs and lug the two extremely large black bags up to our room.

Bright and early the next morning, Charles, Champ and I were up and getting ready for a hot air balloon ride. (Can you believe it? This silly person who couldn't take the height of the Eiffel Tower was going up in a hot air balloon?) Well, when the owner of the company drove up in his somewhat disheveled-looking van, pulling a flatbed with a basket about three feet square on it, I really had second thoughts, and third thoughts, and fourth thoughts. I couldn't back out now, could I? I had been the instigator of this adventure in the first place. Soooo, we drove off to the edge of town, found a nice spot to test the equipment and air currents, and began to fill the balloon with hot air. It never crossed my mind that we would be the crew and have to help get the balloon ready for lift off. The owner/pilot barked out orders, and we followed them as best we could. Charles and Champ unfolded the balloon, stretched it on the ground, and then held it in place while the pilot used a huge fan to blow hot air into it. It frightened me a little when he sent a small balloon into the air and watched its movements for a few minutes, and then said we would need to reverse our planned course. Remember we were on an island (water, water,

Hot Air Balloon Basket.

everywhere and one could easily be blown over the ocean in no time at all). It took nearly an hour to finalize all the preparations and then it was time to fly. My stomach was filled with butterflies; my throat was parched; and my hands were sweaty. Then the pilot told me to get into the basket. Well, getting in was no easy task at age 60! I had to accomplish that feat by stepping into the square opening on the side of the basket and swinging my leg over the edge. It was not pretty, and, certainly, it was not lady-like.

There was room for four and no more. We were literally cheek-to-cheek, with only a small space in each corner for the butane tanks. Slowly, we rose into the air. There was no jerking, no unnerving noise, just a gentle upward motion. I didn't look straight down, but made a concerted effort to look past the other passengers so as to dispel any feelings of vertigo. That worked for a while, but when we rose to 1500 feet and I could see the shadow of our balloon basket on the fields below (about the size of a quarter), I knew I was higher than I really wanted to be.

The pilot was busy every minute of the trip. He had to keep the heat in the balloon and had to steer at the same time. The van was following us on the ground and planned to rendevous with us when we landed, so the pilot had to pick a spot where we would be welcome. (Some of the local farmers were not pleased to have the balloon fly over their land and scare the livestock.) After a couple of hours in the air, we started down and a smile came over my face when the balloon basket shadow begin to get bigger and bigger. At last we found a place to land and we were happy to see the van trailing behind. The actual landing wasn't bad at all. It was soooo good to be on solid ground!

However, the adventure wasn't over yet. We had to straighten out the balloon, fold it back up, and put the basket back on the flatbed. After we finished our chores, the pilot offered us a glass of champagne. It was a tradition, he told us, and we gladly accepted his offer.

Tee-Heeing in Tennessee

Champ's partner, Bob Galligan, hails from McMinnville, Tennessee, and was visiting there with his family in 1988. We were also vacationing in Tennessee and met Bob and his wife, Martha, and their boys in a small town not far from his parents' home. Our children were teenagers at the time and could stay by themselves so when the four of us decided to drive to Lookout Mountain near Chattanooga, they chose to stay at the motel and play tennis instead.

We got a later start that we should have and by the time we drove the 90 miles or so, the sun was setting. The road up the mountain wasn't something we wanted to tackle in the dark, so we headed back down to town for something to eat. Not many restaurants were open that Sunday night and it took us a long time to find one. It took us an even longer time to be served and so the evening hours just vanished.

On the return trip, Bob suggested that his family spend the night in our motel because it was going to be so late when we got back there. Martha agreed to staying over, but insisted she needed to have a least a toothbrush. There were few places open on the interstate highway after 10:00 p.m. but when we finally saw one, we couldn't exit quickly enough to get there. We had to get off at the next ramp and travel about five miles back to the store. It was a very dark night in the hills (no moon at all), and Bob missed the frontage road and drove into the truck weighing line. We had to sit and wait our turn. We were sandwiched in and couldn't get out. It seemed an eternity before we finally drove onto the weighing apparatus. Well, it was more than Martha and I could take! We started to laugh about what the records would show - comparing the weight of our small car to weight of the huge 18-wheelers in front and behind us. We giggled and we giggled. Neither Bob nor Champ thought it as funny as we did. It took another hour to get back to the motel after we got the toothbrush, and neither Martha nor I could quit snickering. The men were silent. It didn't make any difference. We girls just couldn't stop laughing. After we said our goodnights at the motel and went to bed, I had to put my head under my pillow to keep the others from hearing my laughter. Martha was in the next room and she was doing the same. Hee! Hee! Hee!

Even now when we get together and re-tell this story, Martha and I still get tickled and laugh out loud.

Part Three - Travels with Family and Friends

Real de Catorce - 1970

Our first visit to the "Highway of the Kings" outside of Matehuala, Mexico, was in the spring of 1970 when I was five months pregnant with our second son, Matthew. We were traveling with Bobby and Norma Green and their two daughters in a borrowed Scout, and we were pulling a dune buggy behind so we could get to some of the out-of-the-way spots up in the mountains. Ha! You have never seen such an out-of-the-way spot as this one was back then!

Bobby had the coffee brewing just about sun-up and everyone was getting themselves ready for a fun-filled, adventuresome day in the silver mine city of Real de Catorce. Champ had done his homework; he read several books on the history of the area and kept us informed as we traveled toward the mountain. Our destination was only about 26 miles from our hotel, but we had to drive through another small town, then down some very sandy trails, through some dried-up gullies, and then begin our trek upwards on a single lane dirt road. The higher we rose, the more anxious I became. There was no room to pass other vehicles and there was no railing of any kind! The road was rough and extremely bumpy and remember, I was fairly pregnant! Was my baby going to survive this wonderful trip Champ was so eager to take us on? I had my doubts! When we finally reached the top after several hours of very slow, tedious driving, Bobby got out the bunsen burner and proceeded to fix breakfast for us all.

Food didn't interest me, but the men walking out of the tunnel wearing miner's helmets certainly did. Were we going to go through the tunnel? It was how long? A whole mile! It was a dirt tunnel and it had no lights. The only communication between the two ends was a rope with a bell tied on to it, which signaled when someone was starting through the tunnel. About 30 yards into the north end, there was a small inset with a cross and flowers as a memorial to some who had died there. I couldn't believe it was only about 11:00 a.m. and more adventure was ahead of us. I was ready to go home!

Actually the city proper was well worth seeing! We parked in front of the town square and the others all jumped out and scattered off in difference directions. I sat in the car. Champ came back for me several times, encouraging me to come and look at the impressive church, the majestic views, the old headstones in the cemetery. I didn't budge. Not bumping along on the road was all the pleasantry I needed and I just sat there. Norma and the girls were looking for gold nuggets and had a great time in the market place bargaining with the local merchants. Bobby and Champ had discovered some interesting buildings and were really having a good time. Me, too!

As we headed back into the tunnel, I saw several men put on their helmets and walk in behind us. They didn't seem to care that our van would stir up the dust; it was simply their way of life. The trip down was just as bumpy and just as scary, but this time I was sitting on the inside and the sheer drop off wasn't in my immediate view. A hot bubble bath was not waiting for me at the hotel, but a warm shower felt mighty good and the baby was still kicking! Hurray! Thanks again, God.

The Great Southwest - 1971

One of our very good friends, Jimmie Steidinger, owned a small plane and invited us to fly out to Phoenix, Arizona, to visit Bobby and Norma Green, who had recently moved there from Donna. The planning stage was done over a "few drinks" and before I knew it, we were off on a ten-day trip to the great Southwest.

The first inkling of trouble came when we were loading the plane. Jimmie suggested Champ, who weighed about 220 pounds at that time, sit in the front with him so as to offset the weight of the luggage in the back of the plane. Mary, Jimmie's companion, had flown in a single-engine plane on several occasions, but it was the first time for me, and I was more than a little concerned about it.

We were in the air just after sunup and planned to get to Ruidoso to spend the night. There were no real air maps on board to go by, but we did have some photos of quite a few landing strips. Along about Odessa, the clouds began forming a very large thunderhead and we veered off our intended course to avoid it; that took a couple of extra hours. By the time we reached New Mexico, the heat was radiating off the mountains and the plane was reacting to that heat. We bounced and bounced and bounced. Nobody was talking. Mary was biting her fingernails, and there was perspiration beading up on Jimmie's forehead. Prayer was foremost on my mind.

We had to pull out of our first approach to the landing strip and only made the second one by the hair on our chinny, chin, chins. Just after we cleared the tall pines, we had to dive straight down to the runway, and it took every last inch of it for us to come to a complete stop. Thoughts of never going back up in the plane crowded my mind - and this was only the first day of our trip!

The next couple of days were pleasant ones. After we went to the horse races and drove up the mountain to a ski resort, we just relaxed. Then it was time to get on with the trip. Flying over the white sands was incredibly beautiful and I forgot about being scared for a little while.

The Greens, all four of them, were waiting for us in Phoenix. They had their car and their boat loaded for a fishing trip to Guaymas, Mexico, just a couple hundred miles south of the border. It was hot in Arizona but it was even hotter in Guaymas. To make matters worse, our motel accommodations were awful. Bobby and Jimmie slept outside so the girls could share the rooms. The fishing was pretty good and the water was gorgeous. However, when we tried to go ashore for a picnic, we found the beaches full of leaches and so it was back to the boat and back into the sunshine. Everyone was sunburned a little bit and that made the motel sheets feel rougher than ever.

Our foursome decided to cut the fishing trip short and headed back to Phoenix. We were up early and out to the airport for the next leg of trip to Las Vegas, just a short hop and a skip. After we had been in the air for an hour or more, I noticed that there were fewer and fewer cars and buses below (and that some of them seemed to be going faster than we were) so I mentioned it to Jimmie. He talked to someone over the phone and learned we had taken a wrong heading at the airport and were flying over the Mojave Desert. Jimmie quickly turned the plane around. When we landed in Prescott three hours after we left Phoenix, we had only gone about 60 miles from our point of departure. Well, we had lunch and relaxed for a while and then flew on to Las Vegas. Of course, by this time, the heat was coming off the mountains, and we were flying over the Grand Canyon. Yow! Bumping and jerking around over the Grand Canyon put the fear of flying right back in my head - time for prayer! Jimmie assured us that flying with a single engine was safer than with two and that if the one engine went out, we would simply glide down to the ground. The bottom of the Grand Canyon didn't look all that good to me. Anyway, we made it to Nevada and I told Champ that I was definitely not going back up in that plane again!

Las Vegas was exciting and every moment seemed filled with entertainment. We saw several good shows, played the nickel slot machines (I did), and had more than one or two good meals. I had forgotten all about the flight home until it was time to go.

We decided to fly home in two days instead of three, so that meant we would be in the air for long periods of time each day. Two hours into the air, Jimmie needed to find a facility so when we got close to an Air Force base, he just got in their rotation formation, planes at four o'clock, and six o'clock, and eight o'clock, and we landed. Several men in uniform rushed out to see why we were there. They did allow Jimmie to deplane, but none of the rest of us.

When it was time for lunch, we stopped at Deming, New Mexico. It was like something out of a sci-fi movie. There were huge hangars and rows and rows of large aircraft sitting around, but no people to be seen. We were on the ground for fifteen minutes before anyone came by. He directed us to the cafeteria and we had lunch with a handful of airport employees. The big planes were owned by Howard Hughes and they were in mothballs. The whole atmosphere was a little eerie and I was glad to be back in the plane this time.

It was late afternoon by the time we reached Fort Stockton, Texas, but at least there were no heat waves coming off any mountains this time.

I made a dreadful error in judgment by getting up early and having a big breakfast before we started on the last portion of the trip. It was only a few hundred miles back to McAllen, but it seemed a lifetime to me. We weren't in the air but half an hour or so before I knew I was going to have to land somewhere. My lower tract was giving me fits. I tried to maintain my composure, but it was no use. My goose bumps were getting goose bumps. I whispered to Champ that I needed to stop and he just looked at me like I was crazy. There weren't any towns close by and we were flying in thick clouds to boot. Well, pretty soon I didn't care what he said or what he thought. I really needed to be on the ground! Jimmie was kinder than Champ and said he would do his best to find a place to land. Thank heaven for A & M research stations! Jimmie found a landing strip and put the plane on the ground. I made a mad dash for the nearest bush. It wasn't very big, but it was a bush! The rest of the trip was uneventful and I have lived to tell this story on more than one occasion.

France For a Few Francs - 1972

Champ came home one day with a brochure for a trip to Paris, France, sponsored by the Texas Bar Association. The tour included the price of the hotel, the airfare, continental breakfast each day, and one morning of sight-seeing. Total cost from Houston was $249 per person. How could we miss this opportunity? We didn't have much money but, surely, we could come up with that much!

We departed Houston at 11:00 p.m. Saturday evening and arrived in Paris as the sun was rising the next morning. The plane was small and completely filled. Most travelers were businessmen returning from Mexico City. I sat next to the window and Champ was seated next to me. The aisle seat was occupied by a very polite Frenchman who chain-smoked and offered each of us a cigarette every time he lighted one. We both smoked at that time in our lives, but nothing like he did. Dinner was served about 12:30 am. and then there was a period of quiet which lasted several hours. Champ asked me to trade places with him because he couldn't cross his knees and was terribly uncomfortable. I really think it was because each time the man sitting next to Champ reached over to offer us a cigarette, it was evident he didn't use deodorant. What could I say?

Our hotel didn't look quite as nice as the one in the brochure, but it was comfortable enough. The free continental breakfast consisted of café au lait (one/half cup very strong coffee and one/half cup hot milk) and some very hard rolls. You didn't need to have a second cup of coffee; there was enough caffeine in the first cup to last a whole day!

The sight-seeing tour was magnificent. We visited Montmartre, the Eiffel Tower, the Louvre, Napoleon's Tomb, the Arc de Triomphe, and Notre Dame. There was something exciting to see at every turn! Harry's American Bar (Hemmingway's favorite spot) was high on the list of places we wanted to go in Paris so we spent our first evening there. It was a small bar and it was very crowded. It was definitely a smoke-filled room and the only spot we could find to sit was near the back door. Champ struck up a conversation with a very friendly and interesting man from Egypt, who spoke seven or eight languages but not English. They conversed in Spanish most of the rest of the evening, leaving me to watch the crowd.

After a second day of touring the City, we decided to rent a car and tour the surrounding countryside. Our first stop was the Palace of Versailles. The gardens alone were worth the trip to get there.

As we headed toward a dot on the map called Les Andelys, dark clouds began to form on the horizon. That was certainly an omen of things to come! Champ had noticed a small castle just outside the little village and he wanted to drive there. In route, we saw a small town off in the distance (Monfort) and hoped to find a good place to have lunch. The only restaurant there was surprisingly nice. There were quite a few interesting people dining there. One couple had two large dogs with them and another couple were dressed in jodhpurs. The menu didn't have an English translation so Champ relied on me to order our food. (I had taken French at SMU ten years earlier but hadn't said or written a word of it since.) Well, instead of veal, he got liver; instead of avocado salad, he got a whole avocado filled with vinegar; he also got a lot of beets on the side. (Ha! Ha!) I had a good laugh, but he didn't think it was quite so funny! He shuffled the food around on his plate, but only ate the bread which, fortunately, was a long skinny loaf, about 16 inches long.

Back on the road, I began questioning when he thought we might arrive at our destination. I was most anxious to stop before dark and soooo when we crossed the Seine on the outskirts of Les Andelys, we made a short tour of the area and stopped at a quaint hotel. One room cost $8.00 (Doesn't that say it all?). There was a small courtyard where we could park the car and where you could

Thank Heaven for Laughter

watch the barges traveling up and down the river. They weren't the romantic vessels you'd read about in novels; they were homes to those who made their living on the Seine and many had their clothes hanging out to dry.

The dining room was pleasant enough, but the menu was rather limited. Champ didn't trust me to order for him this time, so he ordered an omelette. I ordered ham with mushrooms and that's what I got, but the mushrooms came in a tin can similar to ones you might expect sardines to come in . We chuckled at that, but then the waiter brought out a bottle of wine (which we hadn't ordered) and set it on the table before us. The bottle itself was about six inches in diameter and about five times that tall, and it was an ugly yellow color. We tried not to laugh because the hotel owner seemed so pleased to share his gift with us. However, we did exchange a few smiles during the meal as we raised our glasses.

Our bedroom was interesting. It had a bidet but the water closet and shower were down the hall. Most likely, the bed had been in that room for fifty years or more, and I am sure the mattress/bed clothes had never been changed (washed, certainly, but not replaced.) When we got into bed, we both immediately rolled to the middle and then struggled to keep from squashing one another the rest of the night. When the sun came up the next morning, the castle Champ had read about in the Michelin Guide was in full view out the window of our bedroom.

We hurried to get up and dressed so we could be the first ones at the castle. (Champ doesn't like crowds, except in stadiums.) As we pulled away from the hotel, we saw that there was more to the town than we had first realized. In fact, there were quite a few very nice hotels just blocks away from where we had spent the night! Had we looked a little longer, we might have had more comfortable accommodations but I know we couldn't have had a more memorable stay in that town.

It took about 15 minutes to drive to the castle and we could see the gatekeeper walking up the side of the mountain. He was rather surprised to see us so early, but he let us in. There were only a few post cards to buy and absolutely no literature on the history of the area. I didn't possess enough French vocabulary to ask any pertinent questions, so we looked around and headed back to town to buy a book about the castle. The only one Champ could find was in French (of course), and I spent the next three days trying to translate it.

In no hurry, we opted to have a picnic on the way back to Paris. We bought some cheese, some sliced beef, a long loaf of bread and a small bottle of wine and headed toward the city. We found a nice spot for a picnic and stopped to enjoy our last afternoon in the French countryside. Some locals were having a family gathering nearby and it was good to spend time watching their children at play. Actually, we were missing our children a great deal.

Riding high up in the Eiffel Tower gave me a terrible sense of vertigo I hadn't known before. I always enjoyed acrobatics on the monkey bars when I was a child or diving off the high diving board at the swimming pool (or jumping off the Rio Hondo bridge). This was a new sensation and one I really didn't like. I asked the attendant if I could please ride back down without getting off the elevator and he denied my request. When I stepped off onto the very, very small platform that circled the elevator shaft, I was sure I was going to fall

Dinner at the Lido de Paris.

instantly to the ground. Champ thought I was over-reacting, but was kind enough to help me get around to the descending elevator door. I couldn't allow my eyes to look off into the distance without a real sense of queasiness. When we reached ground level, I told him I would never let myself in for anything like that again. And I haven't, more than six or eight times since then.

We put on our fancy evening clothes the last night in the city and took a taxi to The Lido, one of the world's most famous nightclubs. It was another grand performance: comedic dancers (who left us in stitches), a fine male vocalist, a magician who could actually make a tiger disappear, and the famous dancing girls with glamorous but skimpy costumes. It was all such a wonderful evening until it came time to pay the tab. The second bottle of champagne was not included with the meal and we had just enough cash to get out of there without having to wash the dishes. Traveling by taxi was out of the question, so we strolled the three miles back to our hotel. (This is another one of those funny now, but not so funny then, episodes).

Did we get our $500's worth? Yes, without question. It was a trip to remember! There are still a couple of the inexpensive water colors we bought in Paris, as well as a small oil painting done by one of the local artists at Montmartre hanging on the wall in the middle bedroom of our home.

England on a Shoestring

Our first trip to England together was another one of those inexpensive tours sponsored by the Texas Bar Association. We just couldn't not go; the price was right!

The first day there was filled with sight-seeing some of the places I had visited before and some new ones. We went to the changing of the guard at Buckingham Palace; we stood in line to view the crown jewels; we rode in double-decker buses; we ate fish and chips; we rode in big black taxis; we spent time in the Tate Museum; and we strolled through Hyde Park. What a fascinating city!

It was easier to get around in London than Paris because there was no language barrier (well, almost none). We could actually read and understand most of the street and road signs. So when we decided to rent a car and spend some time in the country, we felt confident it would be simple enough to get behind the wheel and drive anywhere we chose to go. That was rather naive thinking on both of our parts!

Champ drove us to Windsor Castle without much trouble and then we headed on to Oxford. The roundabouts were quite nerve-wracking and having the on-coming traffic on the right, instead of the left side of the road, kept you constantly focused on the road. Did I mention how narrow the roads were? There were no shoulders, none at all.

We were both fairly worn out when we reached Oxford late in the afternoon. Although we didn't have a good map of the city, we did have a general idea of where our hotel was located. Champ decided to duck in behind a bus that was traveling to the heart of town in a lane which indicated that it was for buses only. It wasn't long before a very young bobbie (policeman) pulled us over to the curb, told Champ to get out of the vehicle and proceeded to chastise him for not knowing the English driving laws, for having little or no respect for the English laws, and for behaving as an unwelcome guest in his country. I was sitting in the car, but I could certainly tell by the tone of his voice and the gestures he was making (tapping Champ on the chest with his billy club), the bobbie was determined to berate and embarrass Champ. He certainly did that! Fortunately, our hotel was in the next block and when the bashing was over, we quickly drove to the car park. It was a couple of hours before we even walked out on the street to find a place to have dinner. Champ was ready to get out of town! We set our alarm clock for 5:00 a.m. the next morning and we drove away under cover of dark, hoping to escape the possibility of meeting that young man once again.

It was still very early when we arrived in Stratford-on-the-Avon. We opted to have breakfast at the White Swan Hotel while we waited for the tours of Shakespeare's Home and Anne Hathaway's House to begin. There was only one other couple in the dining room and they spoke in very low tones. When Champ and I started talking, we kept our voices almost to a whisper as well. What a totally different atmosphere from the noisy restaurants back home. People here seemed to go out of their way not to be bothersome or intrusive.

After taking both tours, we headed toward a very small village in the Cotswolds. A high school friend of Champ's, Rene Monday, had married an Englishman and they lived in Naunton, which was not far from Borton-on-the-Water. Rene had cautioned us to call when we got close by, because the only road into town was more or less a one-lane path. Just as we turned down the road, here she came in one of those huge black Austin FX4s (like the London taxis). She had to make a 180-degree turn so we could follow her back to her house. Each township had its own regulations concerning the exterior appearance of its houses, and permission from the council had to be obtained to make any major changes to pre-existing buildings. Rene and Graham had just gotten a big bathtub and had had to remodel their house to accommodate it.

We stayed at a bed-and-breakfast just down the street called The Black Horse Inn. Once again the loo (bathroom) was not in the room, but just down the hall. It was quite interesting to try to sleep right over a pub.

I would like to say that the trip back to London went smoothly, but that was not the case. It started raining early in the day and didn't stop. We drove down to Stonehenge and even got out and walked around a few minutes in spite of the rain. The misty conditions kept us from seeing much of the countryside, and we had to concentrate more on the traffic. The English were used to these driving conditions but we were not. I think we went around on one roundabout (circular intersection) several times before we were sure where to exit. Some drivers were not pleased with our lack of decision-making. However, we managed to get back to the expressway leading into London just before dark.

Champ thought it would be good for me to take a turn at the wheel and soooo I said a little prayer, climbed into the wrong (right) side of the car, and drove the last 40 miles into the city. There were cars darting about on either side of us, but I stayed in my lane and never wavered. I drove just under the speed limit and never looked in any direction, but straight forward. We arrived at our hotel in good order, turned our car into the car park (parking lot), and plopped into our beds. Our hotel was just off of Kensington High Street and there was an elevator train that passed just beneath our window. We didn't hear the train that night; we were exhausted.

There were a great many antique shops along the way to Hyde Park and Champ had fun looking for collector's items to bring home. We found an old pewter plate from the 1800's and a couple of pewter mugs, which became the start of his small but interesting collection. (Someone dropped the plate a few years later and it broke into several pieces but thanks to Super Glue, it still sits on the mantle in our family room.)

When it was time to head back home, we spent quite some time in Harrods looking for something special for the boys. Among other toys, each one received a bobbie's helmet and billy club. Our sons looked much cuter in them than the young man in Oxford!

Bobbies in Donna.

On the Road Again, to Guadalajara!

I was pregnant again in 1974 when we headed south to the interior of Mexico with Beto and Stella Villegas and Dan and Dahlia McKenna. The trip started off with a bang - literally. Since Dan had to work until noon, the rest of us were dropped off at the U.S. Bar and Restaurant in Reynosa to wait for him. We had gone through the immigration process and were biding our time until he could get there. An hour or two went by and I couldn't sit still much longer, soooo I walked several blocks back to the International Bridge just to see if I could spot him in line. Just as I rounded the curve immediately in front of the bridge, a gun shot rang out! Have you ever seen a pregnant woman run as fast as a speeding bullet? I was back in the restaurant in less than two minutes. It seems the police were trying to get someone's attention by shooting in the air. They certainly got mine!

The three-day trip through the central part of Mexico was delightful, except when my husband was behind the wheel. I never thought to criticize the other men's driving, but somehow my own husband needed lots of help in finding the right roads, in making the right turns, and in staying within the speed limit. We traveled through Saltillo, Matehuala, Dolores Hidalgo, and Guanajuato on our way to Guadalajara. We laughed and joked all the way there. What a fun time!

Good friends from Dallas, Happy and Virginia Nelson, and Bobby and Norma Green and daughters were all waiting for us in Guadalajara. We stormed the city. We painted the town red! We shopped until we dropped and then moved on to Puerto Vallarta.

I will never forget the drastic change in scenery from the mountain highway littered with stark volcanic rock formations to the drive along the coast with the tall banana and palm trees growing right out to the water's edge - all within a few hours' drive.

Ah, Puerto Vallarta!!! I had always wanted to go there. It was one of my fondest dreams. It was touted as a very romantic place in all the brochures and we did have a beautiful (small) room with its own (very small) swimming pool. But my experience there was unforgettable for all the wrong reasons - stomach virus, stomach virus, stomach virus! I spent the entire first day in "el bano", sicker than a pregnant lady should be. I begged Champ to get me on a plane and back to Donna, in case the baby came early. My prayers were answered once again when we landed safely at the airport in McAllen.

Mazatlan - 1976

Beto and Stella Villegas drove with our two older boys and us to tour an area of Mexico none of us had seen before. It was an ambitious journey because we had to travel through one of the most arid portions of the country and then we had to cross the Espino de Diablo (Devil's Spine), en route from Durango to the west coast.

Parras was the first stopover on a long, straight road heading west from Saltillo. It was a small wine-producing town and a true oasis to the traveler. There was a nice resort there and we took advantage of it. The boys were glad to be out of the car, and it only took them a few minutes to scamper up the hill just outside our cabin. They weren't gone long before they returned with blood on their hands and scrapes on their knees. Mr. Billy Goat Gruff was at the top of that hill, and I don't know if they teased him or if they didn't even see him, but he took exception to their being there and took out after them. How fast can two boys (6 and 9) come down a hill? Mighty fast, if you don't mind leaving a little skin behind. Fortunately, we had a medicine kit, and their cuts and bruises were tended to properly. They just roamed around the resort grounds after that experience.

The next day's drive was less than exciting for all of us. We drove about 150 miles, without any curves in the road and with no trees or any vegetation to enjoy. Sanborn's Travel Guide provided us with detailed information as to where to go and what to see in Mexico, but didn't say much about this area. It did suggest we stop for lunch at a German restaurant nestled in the piney woods just before we started over the mountain to Mazatlan and so we purposefully did that.

It was well worth the visit. The food was good and the owners were very pleasant.

They allowed the little boys to gather up pine cones and play around in the yard. It was good for them and it was good for us (AND there was no goat nearby).

They advised us not to travel over the mountain late in the afternoon because sometimes the clouds rolled in and the narrow, curvy roads were difficult to drive over in poor weather conditions. It was just after 2:00 p.m. when we set out and the sun was brightly shining. It was picture-perfect weather and we were confident nothing could possibly deter us. The ascent to the top of the mountain was long, very long. The number of miles on the map was no indication of the travel time it took to drive them. Horseshoe curves came one right after the other, and we wound around and around, and made very little progress.

When Beto was driving, I was completely relaxed. After all, he did a lot of driving in his business and I thought he was quite capable of handling the car on those tight curves. Stella, on the other hand, was not so relaxed. She was worried the whole time. When we stopped at a scenic view area to take pictures of the wonderful vistas and to stretch our legs, Champ decided to take a turn at the wheel. I was most concerned now, and Stella began to relax.

I can't remember the distance of the trip, but it was true to its name. The road twisted and turned, and we couldn't see the oncoming trucks, but we could hear them. Thin clouds did roll in, but fortunately for us, they didn't stay long. We arrived at our hotel just as the sun was setting and we all were ready for a margarita (not the boys, of course.)

Champ and Beto lined up a fishing trip in hopes of catching a sail fish. Stella and I declined to tag along. We shopped in the city, instead. Stella loved to shop and could bargain with the best of the vendors. Later, we had a most relaxing time on the harbor tour boat in the afternoon. You can imagine my surprise when we returned to the hotel and Michael came running out to tell us that they had caught three sail fish. I couldn't believe it! It must have been a gag! Then he told me every little detail of how he struggled with his fish and how long it took to get it into the boat. No one could make up a fish story like that, surely not a nine-year old. Champ was as pleased as punch with his catch and Beto smiled all the way home. He was going to hang his trophy in his mother-in-law's restaurant so all the world could see it! Poor Matthew had not had as much fun as the other three. He was a little bit seasick.

The boys had a great time playing on the beach of the Pacific Ocean, but it was quite different from the warm, sandy beaches of South Padre where they normally swam. There were huge rocks at the shoreline and the water was quite cold, but still they managed to enjoy it.

We planned to get an early start on our journey home and we did. It was about 7:30 a.m. when we started up the mountain. I was happy Beto was driving again. In less than two hours we were socked in by the clouds and could not see the road in front of us. Beto had to lower his window and stick his head out, just to see the white line in the middle of the highway. It began to rain. The windshield wipers were going ninety-to-nothing, but he still couldn't see. Now we were all getting anxious. We could still hear the trucks changing gears or braking, but we couldn't see them until they were right in front of us. It was extremely scary and it was still early in the morning.

After a lot of tedious driving, Beto pulled off the road into a small clearing and we decided to wait for the clouds to move away. We sat for quite some time, discussing possibilities before we faced the fact that the clouds might not move at all. What were we going to do about food and water? How dangerous was it for us to sit where we were all day and night? (I began to pray earnestly about how good I would be if I ever got my family off that mountain.) Champ assured me he had his Derringer with him (about the size of a child's toy pistol), and we would be safe. I was not sure that tiny little gun could deter any robber. We sat and I fretted.

The boys were rather enjoying the experience and hoped a black bear or something wonderful like that would come out of the forest. It was possible! Black bears were often seen in the mountains of northern Mexico. However, when a critter did appear, it was a rooster. What a relief! There must have been somebody living near by soooo Beto and Stella ventured out into the fog to find out. They were gone about an hour and I was very concerned about them, but they returned unscathed with a box of homemade breakfast tacos. Ha! Ha! Less than a quarter of a mile away from the car, they had found a small café full of truck drivers smart enough to get off the road in such poor weather conditions. Slowly the clouds began to drift away and we continued our trek over the Devil's Spine without further ado.

Cancun - 1978

Champ loved to travel in Mexico, partly because of the culture and partly because it was relatively inexpensive. He found a small ad in the Texas Monthly magazine offering a magnificent get-away vacation spot near Cancun and was anxious to go there. We booked a cabin on the water's edge and planned to stay a week.

Only when we rented the car at the airport in Cancun, did I get a little concerned. I didn't exactly understand what the agent said when Champ asked for directions to our motel, but it was something like "muy rustico". (He meant that the place was rustic - homely, plain, unpolished, artless, rural, inelegant.) The man knew what he was talking about! It took us quite some time even to find it but when we did, I took one look, started to cry, and pleaded with Champ not to stay there. Everything in the ad was a tiny bit embellished. The laundry hung out on two long clotheslines, chickens scurried around the grounds, and dogs lay close by the screened-in kitchen door. There didn't appear to be any air-conditioning units in the cabins. We lost our deposit but not our vacation.

We found a room at the Villas Tacul motel. What a difference! The two-bedroom villa had two private baths and a large tiled living area and kitchen. There was a small cove for swimming in the ocean and several tennis courts. Each morning the staff would come in and fix breakfast for us with all the trimmings - eggs, ham or bacon, juice, fruit, coffee, and hot bread. I liked this arrangement much better than the first.

Charles and Ann Farris flew in to stay with us and we spent a couple of days exploring the coastal area near Tulum. We looked at the map and decided it wasn't too far to the Mayan ruins of Chichen Itza soooo we headed west through the Yucatan Peninsula. The roads were fairly new but were being overtaken by the jungle. Every now and then we would see someone walking along the road with a gun over his shoulder and a long machete tied to his waist. It was somewhat alarming to me, but Champ said it was for their protection from the wild animals that lived in the region, not for slaying tourists.

We spent the night in an archeological-museum setting. The beds were actually carved-out areas of the walls (quite interesting and not all that uncomfortable). We intended to climb the pyramid first thing the next morning, but it was so humid by 8:00 a.m. we could hardly make it up halfway. There were 91 steps in the staircase leading to the top, and I recall the temperature being just about 91 degrees as well. We were definitely in the jungle and sweltering.

A couple more days in Cancun and we had to leave. Our stay there had been so memorable, we planned a return trip with our children.

Easter in Cancun

We lost no time in planning a return trip to Cancun because we had had such a good time there the year before. Champ's mother and Aunt Helen agreed to join us for the Easter holiday and we rented a six-room villa at Villas Tacul for a week for about $350.

Michael had broken his collar bone just a few days before we left home and had to wear a sling for support. It kept him from enjoying the water as much as he would have liked, but we bought him a small raft at a local shop and he liked that.

Matthew was most interested in snorkeling, and the reef just outside our villa was a perfect place for it. I can still visualize Champ and Matthew - one huge back, one very small back - floating in the water with two little snorkels jutting into the air.

Mitchell was four at the time and he was determined to break open one of the coconuts he had found. He took a small rock hammer and hit it repeatedly until he clawed open his foot, instead of the coconut. It was a holiday weekend and there was no chance of getting a physician to come to the motel, so Champ did some doctoring himself. It was a jagged rip and looked ghastly, and I was sure he needed stitches. However, Champ cleansed the wound and bandaged it carefully. Within a few days, it was completely well. Perhaps the salt water had facilitated the healing process.

Champ's mother and his aunt rode over to Islas de Mujeres with us on a glass-bottom boat and it had entertainers dressed in pirate outfits on board for the tourists.

The ladies played along with their antics, but Mitchell was not too sure about them. The older boys just laughed.

We traveled down to the ruins at Tulum one afternoon and the boys had great fun exploring the area, but the rest of the time was spent on the small beach just out the kitchen door. It was a great place for a family vacation.

Britain, Here We Come!

The Joneses flew en masse from Houston to London in June of 1982. Michael was 14, Matthew was 12, and Mitchell was almost 8. The flight over was long - very, very, long (about 10 hours). We were fortunate enough to have five seats together, but they were in the center of the row so we had to climb over other passengers to get out of our space. That was less than ideal. However, after the dinner meal, the boys settled down and tried to sleep the flight away. Two very small children kept most of us from having any peaceful rest, and it was well past midnight before they finally fell as sleep. Our two younger sons curled up in their seats and put their heads on my lap for the duration of the trip. They were comfortable enough, but it wasn't long before my legs went to sleep. It was a very long flight!

Champ had arranged for Bob Smith, a taxi driver, to meet us at the London airport and drive us into the city. He was waiting at the gate when we arrived and greeted us warmly. He was an extremely nice man and was particularly kind to our sons. As we made our way to the hotel, he pointed out areas of interest and numerous historical buildings. There was a story to go along with each place and he directed most of his conversation to the children. They liked him already.

We arrived at the Kensington Palace Hotel, had a bite to eat, and fell into bed. We slept through the rest of the morning and well into the afternoon. After a stroll in Hyde Park, we took a taxi to The Beefeater by the Tower of London for a medieval dinner. It was all fun and games for the tourists, but Mitchell was not going to smile one minute no matter how hard the court jester or the other entertainers tried to cheer him up. No, and he didn't like the food, either! Perhaps seven was a little young for this sort of thing or perhaps it was the jet lag, but the older boys enjoyed it immensely.

Champ dropped his eye glasses and broke one of the lenses during the evening performance. The next morning we set out to find a place to get them repaired. We found a shop not too far from our hotel and were told we would have to wait about an hour for them to prepare the lens and adjust the new frames. Michael was anxious to be on his own for a while and asked if he could meet us back at the hotel. I was dubious about his going off alone, but Champ reminded me that Mike was almost 15 and could take care of himself. He could speak the language, couldn't he? What could possibly happen to him? Well, Michael crossed the street and went into a small mall with lots of smaller shops inside.

When he came back out to the street, he turned the opposite direction of our hotel. He walked nearly a mile before he realized nothing looked familiar and so he hailed a taxi. I think the fare back to our hotel was only one pound (less than $2), but Mike tipped him twice that much. I had been very concerned that Mike wasn't back at the hotel within a reasonable period of time, but Champ assured me that I was over-reacting. Just the same, Mike and I were both pleased to be reunited.

We took the boys to see "84 Charring Cross

London Visitors - Three Boys and Camille.

Road" in the theater district that evening, and the older boys seemed to enjoy it. Mitchell, on the other hand, fell asleep during the first act and woke during the intermission. He didn't see us standing at the back of the theater so he crawled up next to the lady sitting on the other side of us. He was really unhappy the boys had gotten ice cream during the break while he was left all alone with some stranger.

A trip to London without a trip to Harrods was unthinkable. Every toy in the world was available there. Mitchell got army soldiers to play with and Matt got a Sherlock Holmes hat. Michael was more interested in tennis gear, and had fun looking at all the rackets and clothing the players were wearing at Wimbledon. We even had lunch there in one of their famous restaurants.

Scotland was just a train ride away and we boarded the Royal Highlander for an overnight trip to Inverness. The travel brochure didn't mention the many stops the train made, but there were quite a few. The three sleepers were adjacent to one another but someone had to sleep in the single compartment so I got to spend the 10 hours riding alone.(It wasn't all that bad.) I did have to make a trip or two down the train car to the water closet but there were not very many other passengers so it wasn't much of an ordeal. Thirty minutes before we arrived at the train station the next morning, we were treated to scones and hot tea. What a nice tradition! The boys loved the scones.

It took two taxis to get all of us and our luggage to Dunain Park, where we were welcomed with coffee, tea, chocolates, and cookies. The boys ate everything in sight and set out to explore the premises. They were only gone a short while before the telephone rang and our host informed us that our boys had overstepped the boundaries. They had been chased by some neighboring long-horned sheep and had strayed onto someone else's property. Most inappropriate behavior! We would have to keep a tight rein on them.

Well, we managed to entertain them with croquet and badmitton and a lot of chocolate bars, but we were all glad to be on the road to the Isle of Skye the next afternoon.

The sun did not go down until about 11:00 p.m. in northern Scotland during the summer months and it rose shortly after 3:00

a.m. That made for a very long day! Most bedrooms, however, were equipped with long, heavy drapes to keep out the light so you could sleep in relative darkness.

Luggage for five was always a problem for us. Even the boys had to dress (slacks and coats) for dinner in the nicer inns in Scotland so they had to have lots of changes of clothes. We rented a small station wagon for our trip around the area but we could barely see out for all the gear we had. Fortunately, there was very little traffic on the country roads. Mike and Matt had recently seen "Smokey and the Bandit Part II" at the movies and took great pleasure in saying, "Take a right turn, Daddy, and you'll be in the clear" over and over again when we had to make a decision about directions. They laughed and laughed. Champ didn't think it was quite so amusing.

We drove along Loch Ness for several hours and never saw the monster, but we did see a bagpipe player performing at one of the roadside parks. The boys were interested in knowing what he wore under the kilt, but the piper didn't say, and they didn't dare look.

The Skeabost House Hotel on Skye was a haven for the boys. They could scamper around the grounds and over the rock walls, and not bother a soul. There was a miniature golf course right next to the inn and they loved being outdoors. We took a boat trip out to see some baby seals and toured a local castle. It was cold and windy on the island, but we bundled up and weathered the weather.

We had scheduled a lovely evening meal at Skeabost House and while we were waiting for our seating, we had an opportunity to chat with the wife of a local Episcopal minister. She mentioned something about "chicken bosoms" being on the menu and we Texans didn't quite make the connection between bosoms and breasts at first. Then we all had a good laugh. We still mention "chicken bosoms" from time to time.

There was a small single track (dotted line) road that led back to Inverness and Champ insisted we take that one instead of retracing our route. It was the smallest, loneliest road I had ever traveled. It was just as advertised: room for one car only. If you met another vehicle, you had to find the widest spot in the road and inch around one another. We only encountered a couple of cars in the 60-mile drive - that was plenty.

At the end of that day's journey was a most wonderful resort. Strathgarve was perfect for the Jones family. The innkeepers greeted us with more scones and tea, and encouraged us to stay for as long as we liked. They had three large dogs, Sledge, Thunder, and Flash. They were all very friendly animals and seemed to take a liking to our three boys right away. Our rooms were quite a distance from the main lobby and Mitchell had an enormous bathtub adjacent to his bedroom. He must have spent three hours in there playing with the toy soldiers we bought at Harrods. He was happier there than anywhere on the entire trip.

I asked if we could possibly get some of our clothes washed by the staff and they agreed to do our laundry. Naturally, they charged by the article. When the bill came back, I was not surprised that it totaled nearly $100, because every single thing the boys had brought to wear had been worn at least once, and there were over a hundred pieces of clothing. The only concern was that none of the articles had been ironed.

Mike and Matt had a "chantilly lace" dessert the first evening, which consisted of a lightly baked meringue filled with chocolate pudding and topped with lots of whipped cream. It was the <u>creme de la creme</u> for them. We never had to coerce them to get dressed for dinner after that.

It was still light outside after dinner, so the boys had time to roam around the grounds. The dogs enjoyed tagging along, sometimes chasing the many bunny rabbits that made their appearance just before dark. The long hours of daylight helped deplete the boys' energy, and they were always ready for a good night's sleep when the sun finally went down.

The innkeeper was quite a fisherman and offered to let us fish in a specially designated area for guests of the hotel. We didn't have the proper gear, and he was gracious enough to let us borrow his tackle. None of us had ever been fly fishing, but the proprietor gave us a quick lesson and a few tips. It was terribly cold that day (overcast and misty), but it was the only day we were going to have there, soooo off we went. We fished and we fished. We caught nothing. We ate the picnic lunch the hotel had packed for us. We fished and we fished. We caught nothing. Matthew fished so hard, he threw the best lure we had over to the opposite side of the river. Champ insisted Matt swim across to retrieve the lure, and he nearly froze to death in his wet warmups.

After our return to Dunain Park, we scheduled another fishing trip, but it was not any more fruitful. We were admonished by the local water bailiff for fishing in the wrong spot, and were asked to leave the premises. It wasn't our best outing. Michael fell into the water this time.

The train ride back to London was uneventful but plenty of adventure lay ahead. Wimbledon was in its second week and we planned on seeing some of the matches. The first trip out to the grounds was by taxi. It was a bit expensive, but we wanted to get there in time for the first matches and we didn't have any tickets. There was a long waiting line when we arrived, but it didn't take long to gain entrance to the grounds. Back then, each of the main courts had a "standing area" where you could see the match without having a ticket. Luck was on our side, and we got to see Jimmy Connors and John Lloyd in their separate performances. It was a marvelous (and inexpensive) afternoon of tennis. Michael left us from time to time to see who else was playing, and came back with tales of the play going on at several of the other courts. He had seen Chrissy Evert and was very impressed.

The next day Champ decided to buy Wimbledon tickets on the "black market" and spent quite a few dollars to get Center Court seats. Of course, we couldn't get five seats together so Champ and Mitchell took the best seats at mid court (the fifty yard line), Mike and Matt sat on the east side about ten rows up from the court, and I sat by myself on the west side, up under the overhang.

We watched a match between two relatively unknown players and I watched my family more than the match. Champ and Mitchell were just behind some extremely well dressed people and before the match was well underway, the lady turned and handed Mitchell some candy. He gladly accepted her kind offer and before long, put his head down and went to sleep. I could just envision the photographers on the opposite side picking him out of the crowd and zooming in on his lack of interest in the contest. On the other side of the stadium, I could see the older boys crouching down, waiting to make an exit when the players exchanged ends. I didn't know where they were going, but I was mighty glad to see them return to their seats before too long an interval. I was fairly sure no one would kidnap them at Wimbledon, but one's thoughts do run wild every now and then.

We were staying at the Royal Horseguards Hotel on our return to London and the doorman there bore a strong resemblance to one of our dearest friends and hunting camp buddies, Andrew Champion. He and the boys became friends right away. They were really enjoying the trip, even Mitchell. We spent the day shopping for friends and family at home and found a few items for ourselves. During our walk through St. James' Park, Mitchell spied a pigeon being hounded by several larger birds, and he took off in a hurry to save it. Onlookers mistook his behavior and thought he was trying to kill the pigeon. His brothers remarked (rather loudly) that he probably wanted to cook it for dinner. We smiled, but no one else did.

Bob Smith picked us up and returned us to the airport in good fashion. He talked with the boys and asked them about their trip and even stopped his car to buy them some Jelly Belly candy. He couldn't have made a better impression on all of us soooo when we traveled to England several years later, we asked him to meet our plane once again.

Here Come the British!

The Swallow family came to Texas for a business venture in 1985 and have been coming back every year since. Business brought our two families together, but pleasure has kept us very close friends through the years.

Our children were all teenagers when we first met and they had great fun getting acquainted with each other and our differing lifestyles. Heidi, Chris and Nicki (twins) went to boarding school miles away from home; our boys went to school right down the street. Their son played field hockey; ours played football. They spoke English; we spoke American. They lived in the rain and cold weather; we lived in the heat and dry weather. In spite of the many differences, we found lots of fun in spending time together.

One August we escorted them to some of the more interesting areas in our part of Texas. We drove to Fredericksburg and visited the Nimitz Museum; stopped for a quick visit to Luckenbach (didn't see Waylon and the boys, but bought a tape of Willie's song and played it over and over in the car until everyone knew all of the words); traveled over to Austin and showed them the Capitol; spent several nights in San Antonio seeing the sights - the Alamo, the Riverwalk and the Texas Folklife Festival. It was 100 degrees in the shade and the Brits were feeling the heat, but it didn't keep them from enjoying the trip. On Christmas day that year, we had a phone call from England. The Swallows were having a party at their home and wanted to wish us a happy holiday. After a few words of cheer, their whole crowd of guests burst into "Luckenbach, Texas". What fun!

The Swallows happened to be in town during the spring of Matthew's senior year and they all came to see him run in the finals of the district track meet. They arrived just after noon and had to stay late because Matt ran early in the 400-meter race and then again in the mile relay, which was the last event of the day. Chris timed every race and enjoyed the whole experience. When Matthew's team ran, they came in third and missed out on a trip to the regional meet. Matt sank to the ground in bitter disappointment. Chris jumped the fence and crossed over the track to where Matt was sitting and said, "Jolly good show, Matt! That was YOUR fastest time ever!" A smile crept over both their faces.

Tony and Helga and Champ and I have traveled many places together (Spain, Mexico, Switzerland, Big Bend), and have wonderful memories. We have stayed in fancy places and we have stayed in some rather "rustic" ones. We have had to be flexible on more than one occasion and that's what has kept us laughing so much of the time.

The most memorable event for me was Tony's fiftieth birthday celebration in London in 1990. The Swallows had invited us to Wimbledon for the day, beginning with a champagne brunch before the first match. I was pleased to see so many of their friends whom we had met before and I was totally impressed with the setting. A tent large enough to accommodate several hundred guests had been erected just across the grounds from the main entrance and we enjoyed a five-course meal inside of it. Each table was set with fine china and elegant silverware and was adorned with a huge floral arrangement. Background music was provided by a gentleman sitting at a white grand piano. The food was excellent and the conversation better. What a birthday party!

Some of Tony's guests didn't bother to watch the tennis matches, but I was an avid fan of Ivan Lendl and didn't want to miss a stroke of his match. I couldn't tear myself away from the match, even when it was time for tea and scones back at the tent.

The Jungles of Campeche - 1979

One summer we traveled to Mexico to visit Dr. "Pepe" Armora at his ranch in the jungles of Campeche, located in the Yucatan Pennisula. It wasn't easy to get to Cuidad de Carmen, but we flew into Mexico City, stayed overnight, and took a small plane to Veracruz. Then we traveled by car along the coast until we reached our destination. The drive was beautiful. We saw lush palms trees lining the oceans's edge and exclaimed over the gorgeous deep blue water. It was a very relaxing trip, and most pleasing to the eyes.

Ethel Armora was waiting for us at her brother's house and we spent the first night visiting with her family there. They talked (in Spanish, of course) and laughed at one another's jokes. Champ understood most of the conversation, but I didn't. Yet when they laughed, I laughed. It was just a means of participating in the fun.

Off to Sabancuy the next morning, we arrived at mid-day to find that the accommodations we were supposed to stay in had not been prepared for us. In fact, the summer house had been closed up for quite some time and it would have been impossible for us to stay there overnight. When I saw the double hammock that was to be our bed, I wasn't too disappointed.

We had lunch at a very small café with a dirt floor and only two tables for customers. The proprietor owned several chickens and they walked through the room while we were eating. At first I was concerned about what I was going to eat and the possible effect it might have on me at a later date, but Ethel assured me that anything on the menu would be okay. I think Champ had some local dish, but

I played it safe and had soup and crackers. Would you believe that it was exceptionally good soup? Would you believe the owners were most gracious hosts? Although they didn't have much, they offered all the hospitality they had. What a nice experience!

Four hours later we were on the last leg of our journey to the ranch. We had just turned off the main highway and onto what had previously been a dirt road. Now it was nothing but mud puddles and deep ruts. It was the wet season and it had been seriously raining the whole week prior to our arrival. We drove within a mile or so of the camp before we got stuck in mud. The ranch foreman had to pull us the rest of the way with the tractor. If it was this difficult to get into the ranch, how were we ever going to get out?

The camp building itself was quite nice. It was made of concrete block with a large family/dining area and two large bedrooms with a shower bath in between. There were no beds. Hammocks (for one) were strung up in each bedroom and I chuckled to myself when I noticed them. I had never slept in a hammock overnight, but at least I wouldn't be sharing one with Champ! Well, it was an experience of a lifetime.

Getting into a hammock was fairly easy. Getting the blanket arranged was quite something else. If I put the blanket on the bottom, I froze on the top side. If I put the blanket on the top, I was sweating underneath it, but my bottom was very cold. Sandwiching yourself in between was quite a trick. I had a great laugh at my own struggles, but when Champ tried getting into his hammock, I nearly fell out of mine. After we turned off the lights, I remembered some of the stories the men had been telling about bugs and spiders. Immediately I envisioned scorpions and tarantulas falling from the ceiling into the hammock with me. I didn't fall asleep for a very long time. Champ, however, was peacefully snoring away before long.

The next day it rained some more, but Dr. Armora was determined we have a good look at the ranch while we were there, so his cowboys brought horses for us to ride. I was not exactly an experienced rider, but thought I could stay up with the rest of them so I went along. When we got to the dense jungle area, the ground was more than saturated. Water was almost stirrup-high. Needless to say, the horses were not happy to be plodding along in that soooo when my horse simply refused to go any farther; one of the cowboys had to lead it by the reins. What a picture!

Stories were often told about the jaguars that lived in the area and I was on the look-out every minute we were in that jungle. The men carried on conversations (in Spanish, of course) and laughed every so often. I wasn't laughing; I was praying I would live long enough to get back to my hammock.

The good food and good fellowship made the trip a success.

San Miguel Allende via Real de Catorce

Champ had always wanted to travel with the boys in Mexico, and Real de Catorce was only a few hours away. I was most reluctant to go again (for a variety of reasons) but finally agreed. We spent the first night in Monterrey, which was only 150 miles south of the border. Due to the enormous amount of traffic, it was difficult to get to the hotel but we managed. However, when we were trying to get to Horsetail Falls just outside the city the next day, we became miserably lost. Finally, we hailed a taxi and gave the cabbie $10 to lead us to the correct road. All three guys (Champ, Matt, and Mitch) were embarrassed to have to ask for help, but I was thankful they did.

We took the tour of the falls and then headed towards Real de Catorce. It was mid to late afternoon when we started up the mountain and I was hoping we could stay in Mateguala and set out early the next morning. No dice. What could possibly happen to us? I was terribly anxious until we got to the top, even though the road was much improved. I knew we still had to go through that unlit tunnel and I didn't want to do it after dark.

There was still a little afternoon sun left when we reached the town center. The steep up-hill/down-hill streets were difficult to navigate, even at a slow pace. We hit something in the road and immediately the "check engine" light came on. I was ready to call it quits and go home but the others weren't.

Our reservations were at a motel on the far side of the city and the sun was setting just as we arrived at our destination. The parking lot was part of a steep hill just north of the motel, and when we stopped the car, a young man came out and put a large rock behind each of the tires. I wasn't sure that would have prevented the car from rolling backwards, but it was dark now. I just wanted to get to the room and relax. Well, the accommodations were adequate; there was a single light bulb in the middle of the room; there were two bed-like structures formed out of rock with a straw mattress and a woolen blanket on each; and there was a curtained area for changing clothes and taking a shower. It was too late to think about not staying, soooo we brought in our luggage and settled in for the night.

The owner/manager served our supper in the dining room and, although it was quite modest, it was good. The rum and coke was even better. I tried not to complain, but Champ could see the disappointment in my face and actions. What had he gotten us into this time? Matthew and Mitchell were taking it all in stride and even laughing at me, but the next morning, they had a story of their own to tell. A cat had come through the transom on the door of their room during the night and had jumped on one of them.

He yelled and that scared the other one, and he yelled. They didn't get much sleep after that. It was my turn to laugh this time!

A quick look around the town and we were gone. We sailed down the mountain, across the valley, and into the heavy traffic on the road to San Luis Potosi, with the "check engine soon" light still glowing. I suggested we get the engine checked out, but there wasn't time. We needed to be in San Miguel de Allende before nightfall and that was several hundred miles down the road. The scenery flew by.

Matthew learned to drive like the Mexican truckers in no time at all. He drove right up behind a truck, waited a few minutes and then passed it, going as fast as the car would go. My heart was in my throat most of the time, but I didn't scream or anything.

San Miguel de Allende was like an oasis, compared to the previous day's travel. The weather was cool, the hotel was very comfortable, and the food was excellent. I could have stayed there several days, but we had lots of sight-seeing to do and needed to return to Texas the very next day. We visited the old churches, the town square. and the antique shops. It was a most enjoyable day.

Then it was back in the car (with the "check engine soon" light still on) for a very long drive home. It wasn't until we crossed the border in Reynosa that the light suddenly went out. The boys teased me about being so jittery over nothing for a long time after that.

Two days later, Champ went in for open-heart surgery. It should have been me!

San Miguel de Allende Revisited

Charles and Flo Kennedy took us to San Miguel about eight years ago for a long weekend, and the trip was nothing like the first. We didn't race to get there, but took our time and enjoyed the scenery. After arriving at our lovely hotel, we sat out on the terrace, enjoyed the music and sipped a few drinks. It was a most relaxing trip.

Sight-seeing was on the agenda for the next day and we re-toured some of the churches and shops we had seen with the boys. We spent some time in one of the museums and wiled away the afternoon looking for antiques. We had dinner at a restaurant overlooking the city and that was a highlight of the trip. How enjoyable!

Talovera (hand painted china) was all the rage in the border gift shops and we were not far from a small town where it was hand crafted. We stopped at one of the kilns and looked on, as the young people made bowls, saucers, platters and pitchers. It was most interesting to watch the teenagers paint the earthenware. Each design represented a different family. Charles and Flo bought 12 place settings and so did we. Our dishes immediately went to the deer lease for special entertaining.

A police officer stopped us for running a stop sign in San Luis Potosi, but consented to a monetary gift (bribe), instead of a fine. It took some haggling and about an hour of our time, but it was worth not having to follow him downtown to the police station. The rest of the trip to Matequala was pleasant and we had a very good dinner in the restaurant there.

Champ had looked carefully at the map of northen Mexico and had discovered a different route we could take home. Of course, we had to get up early and get on the road because he was so excited about seeing new territory. Instead of turning east at Galeana, we took a small road (dotted lines on the map) north over the mountain. It was only about 17 kilometers (10 miles), but it took us three hours to get over the top and down the other side to Rayones.

I was concerned as soon as we left the city proper. The dirt road became more and more narrow and the incline steeper and steeper. We only passed one on-coming car and absolutely no one was headed in the same direction we were going. There was a fork in the road at one spot, but there were no signs to indicate where each road led, so we just guessed and continued on. We passed a small shrine on the side of the road with two crosses, and it occurred to me that it might be the last sign of civilization we would see for awhile. I was right! There were no houses on the mountaintop, no visible sign of life (not even cattle), and the telephone pole lines had dwindled down to a single strand. Charles was driving his Chevrolet Suburban and it was almost as wide as the trail we were on.

Talking had all but stopped. The curvy, winding road demanded Charles' full attention. At times you couldn't see where the road was turning before you got there. We reached the half-way point and no one spoke of turning back. Flo didn't seem overly anxious, but Champ wasn't talking, so I knew he was apprehensive about the rest of the trip. I was silently praying. After driving about 45 minutes in silence, we finally met an on-coming vehicle. It was great to see other travelers, but the road was really full of potholes now and there was just barely enough room for us to inch by one another. They seemed rather surprised to see us; I suppose they hadn't seen many Suburbans up on that mountain road.

Well, as time passed, the road seemed to be getting wider, with fewer potholes, and it looked as though we were actually going to survive this ordeal. It was just a little after 2:00 p.m. when we arrived in Rayones and we stopped at the first restaurant we came to for food and something to drink. Hallelujah! Talk about an oasis!

The last 150 miles to the border were on a paved road and were uneventful. Thank heaven.

New York City with the Girls - 2002

My sister, Eloise, my daughter-in-law, Melissa, our good friend, Hollie Kirby, and I took a long weekend trip to New York City. All of us had been there at one time or another, but this time was exceptional. The city was still reeling from the 9/11/01 terrorist attack and the arms of the tourist business were open wide to any and all who would venture their way. We stayed at a hotel on 48th Street for less than $100 a room and had little or no trouble getting tickets to Broadway plays, hailing taxis, or finding space at most restaurants.

We were in and out of taxis all day every day while we were there and some of our most amusing incidents happened in them. Eloise had retired from the teaching profession, but never retired from taking an interest in people. She always sat in the front seat of the cabs (she needed to use a cane due to knee problems) and immediately struck up a conversation with each driver we encountered. Many of the cabbies were not locals and many could barely speak English, but it didn't matter to Eloise. She was interested enough to question them about their background, their length of stay in the states, and their reasons for coming to America. Surprisingly enough, they didn't seem to mind talking with her and seemed to almost appreciate her asking.

When our plane landed at noon on Thursday, Eloise, Melissa, and I burst into "New York, New York" before we even got to the baggage claim area. We were ready for fun and laughter! Hollie arrived about half an hour later and we converged on the city. We took a taxi to the hotel and spent a few moments checking in and getting ready for our first outing in the "Big Apple". The primary objective of the trip was a visit to the site where the twin towers had stood just a few months before. We had to purchase tickets to get into the long line that waited each day to pay its respects to the fallen Americans who had worked and died there or had lived close by. We were fortunate enough to get tickets for that very afternoon and, after milling around the area for several hours, we took our places in line. I cannot describe the scene without tears welling up in my eyes. It was such a vast area, such total destruction, such an emotional experience for all who walked by the viewing area. The walls were polka-dotted with good graffiti, poems, odes, flowers, photos of missing loved ones, and American flags. It was simply overwhelming! Yet, there was a sense of togetherness - one which bonded all of us into a particular people - Americans, one and all.

My heart was saddened for those lost, but encouraged by the resulting regard people were expressing for one another and the devotion they expressed for our country. People on the sidewalks of New York were quite different in their demeanor than their reputation belied. They seemed kind, polite, and caring.

It was nearly dark by the time we arrived at the hotel, and it seemed to me that we would be foolish not to take advantage of the short time we had in the city to do a little more sight-seeing. We jumped out of one taxi and hailed another to take us to the Empire State Building. Our timing couldn't have been better. Few people were standing in line at 9:00 p.m. to take the elevators to the top, but we were there. We waited less than ten minutes for our tickets and were on our way up in no time. It wasn't until we reached the end of the first elevator ride that I remembered how badly I hated to be that high in the air.

I had forgotten that we had to change elevators and ride up another few floors. My heart wanted to find an escape route but none was available. Soooo I just pretended it didn't matter and went right on up to the tippy top. What a view!!! Melissa looked over the wall and was horrified to see people walking on the street below, looking about the size of ants. She was totally taken aback. I knew better than to look straight down and spent my time looking way out over

Thank Heaven for Laughter

the water at Ellis Island, the Statue of Liberty, and Staten Island, all beautifully lit and glimmering in the night. It was better than in the movies! (Yes, we looked for the teddy bear by the telescope, but it wasn't there.)

Friday morning we were up and moving early. We stepped across the street to the Expresso Cafe for breakfast and had fun watching the locals hurry in for a 24-ounce cup of coffee and a bagel or two on their way to work. Many were wearing tennis shoes, but carrying dress shoes to put on later. What a different life style to ours in laid-back South Texas!

We took a taxi to Radio City Hall and took the guided tour. It was great fun for me because I had been there a couple of times as a young girl - way back in the late 40's and early 50's. There were plenty of changes during those many years, but some of the basic themes had remained the same. The Rockettes still performed, although not as frequently as in the past. The grandeur was still there but it was beginning to fade.

How fortunate I was to have seen the majesty of the earlier days! (Once when I was about ten, my mother took me to see a movie at Radio City Hall. When I went out to the concession stand and asked for a box of popcorn, the attendant replied, "And just what part of the South are you from?" I couldn't imagine how someone could know I was from the South until I listened to the next person [a New Yorker] ask for something. It was almost another language!)

We walked to Rockefeller Center and then down a side street to a fire station where we spent some time with men who had been involved in the rescue operations of 9/11. One of the firefighters had actually lost a brother that terrible day. It was important for us to listen to their stories and to offer our concern and friendship.

Lunch at the Ellen's Starlight Diner was a novelty. The waiters and waitresses sang and everyone enjoyed music from the "good old days." It was like being in an old malt shop but with several hundred people.

We taxied down to the pier and took the ferry across to Staten Island and back before we headed to the hotel room. Eloise and I decided to rest a little bit while Mel and Hollie went shopping for themselves and their families. We met up again in plenty of time to get ready for dinner before the theater and we were right on time for the curtain of "42nd Street." My toes were tapping right away and everyone enjoyed the performance immensely. We thought we lost Eloise during the intermission, but she had gone upstairs to the ladies' room and couldn't get back quickly enough for the second act curtain.

Saturday morning was busy. We walked to one of the television studios to see if we could get on one of the early morning shows but we were too late. We walked past Times Square to a restaurant that my cousin, Eloise Nowak, had patronized for years but which was no longer there. We walked past a Maytag truck and stopped in our tracks. Well, there was at least one Maytag repairman working in this world, and we caught him in the act in New York City. Actually we caught him with our camera when he came out of the building. He laughed right along with us when we asked if we could take his picture.

Another taxi ride took us to Central Park later in the day and we laughed until our sides felt as though they were going to split open. Just as we approached a traffic light, a horse-drawn carriage pulled up beside us and the horse looked into my open window. Our noses were only a few inches apart. Mel looked at the horse and asked, "Why the long face?" Even the cabbie had to laugh at that. We tried to have dinner at The Tavern on the Green, but we didn't have reservations and not nearly enough money to get in without them.

It had just begun to rain so we asked the cab driver to take us for a tour of Central Park. He obliged us with a 30-minute ride. When he dropped us off at a Starbucks close to our hotel, he got out of the cab and took our photo as we were kicking up our heels and singing "Singing in the Rain"! He remarked that we were the friendliest passengers he had ever had in all his years as a cabbie. Of course, he earned an extra big tip for that statement.

Dinner in Chinatown was one more interesting event. The food was superb and we had a great time using chop sticks and tasting a variety of dishes. When it was time to leave, we asked the owner to get us a taxi. In a few minutes an unmarked car drove up in front of the restaurant and honked. It didn't look much like a taxi to us and it didn't have a meter but we decided to ride along anyway. This was the only driver that Eloise couldn't talk to. He only spoke Chinese. He knew his numbers in English and convinced us that he could get us to our hotel. Thank heaven, he did.

Sunday morning we were up bright and early so we could attend the first service at St. Patrick's Cathedral. We were all impressed with the interior of the building (paintings, statuary, and architecture). We were also impressed when Beverly Sills, the opera star, was ushered into a nearby pew.

Our last taxi ride was to the airport and our adventure was over. What fun we had in the "Big Apple"! What a lot of laughs! Hollie remarked in a note to me later that she hadn't laughed so much in her entire life as she did that weekend.

North Zulch, Texas - 2005

I need to get this down on paper because I'm afraid I might forget some of the details and they are what make this adventure so special.

We were trying to get to East Texas for the funeral of a beloved family member, Champ's niece, and in our haste to get some of the mileage under our belt, we left Donna about mid-afternoon on Thursday. We had not gone 20 miles north of town until I was pulled over and given a ticket for speeding. I was guilty. I had no recourse, but to accept the citation and get on with the journey. It was not an auspicious beginning to the trip. Probably it was an omen, though.

It was getting dark as we approached Victoria and we took what I thought was a shortcut to the highway to Bryan. It was a long cut, if anything, and I had to deal with lots of construction and two-way traffic on narrow roads for several hours. We drove by several small towns which didn't have any motel/hotel accommodations soooo when we finally arrived (about 8:30 p.m.) in one that did have a motel, I drove right into the parking lot and asked Champ to please let us stop for the night. There was room in the inn and we ventured down the street for dinner. Everything seemed to be working out nicely. During the night I was awakened by the sound of two snorers. One was coming from the bed next to me and one was coming from the person on the other side of the wall. It was almost rhythmic - one snore here, another snore there, here a snore, there a snore. Ha! Ha! Ha! I couldn't stop giggling.

Thank Heaven *for* Laughter

We were up early and on the road before 8:00 a.m. I had coffee in the room so we were not in a hurry to stop for breakfast. (Champ always likes to stop where there are lots of cars, indicating how good the locals like the place, or where there are no cars at all, indicating a new adventure.)

It was mid-morning before we found just the right spot and it turned out to be a new adventure. The owner was also the waiter and cashier and although he was very friendly, he didn't have much to offer on the menu. Nothing Champ asked for (pancakes, bacon, orange juice, coca cola) was available. They had just run out, so he told us. He did have coffee and he did have eggs so guess what we decided to have for breakfast.

It wasn't far from there to North Zulch, a tiny town north and east of Bryan. After the service was over, we headed back toward Austin. We stopped for dinner at a famous barbeque restaurant in Taylor. It was just about 6:00 p.m. when we got there and much to our dismay, they were just about to close for the evening. We ate quickly and left.

It seemed too early to stop for the night, so I suggested we head back to Interstate 35 and take the big highway, instead of the small roads making a loop around Austin. Big mistake on my part! The closer we got to the Austin area, the more traffic there was. It was getting dark and I couldn't make out the highway signs until it was too late to make a change in directions. We got in a turn-only lane and headed away from the expressway and into lots of construction. Champ had a few comments to make which were not well received, and we traveled on in silence. After about 20 minutes of driving away from our intended path, a U-Haul trailer pulled out in front of me and I decided to follow it wherever it led me. I needed an angel and here it was! It went through the traffic light; I followed. It turned onto the interstate; I followed. (No one in his right mind would cut in front of someone who was following a U-Haul, would he?) I followed that vehicle for 30 miles - from the north side of Austin to Buda - without ever getting out of my lane. The traffic slowed to a stand-still a couple of times, but the U-Haul and I were in it together and I was feeling rather good about it all. Champ was not so pleased. (Our 41st wedding anniversary was coming up in just a few days and I began to wonder if we were going to make it.)

It was after 9:00 p.m. before we reached San Marcos where there were plenty of motels but few available rooms. The only one we could find was over-priced and on the second floor. Champ opted not to stay, soooo we drove on to Seguin. There was a very nice motel on the outskirts of town. We found a room there and settled in for the night. I don't remember our talking much but I think he finally did kiss me goodnight.

Dinner at Dripping Springs - 2005

Our very good friends, Jimmie and Barbara Steidinger, live in Donna most of the year but bought some ranch land just outside of Dripping Springs about ten or twelve years ago and spend part of their time there as well. It is about a 325-mile drive from one place to the other. They have built a lovely home there with a fantastic view of the surrounding hills and enjoy having guests come to visit them. They have made friends with quite a few of the local folks and like to include them when they have a party.

Just the other day, Jimmie called to say he and "Bubba" were going to have a party on Friday night. Some long-time friends of his from Louisiana were driving over to cook jambalaya and Jimmie had hired a Cajun band from Austin to be the entertainment. He wanted us to be there. We already had obligations for Saturday evening, but we decided it would be nice to spend some time with old friends so we spent a few hours at the office, jumped into the car and headed north to the Hill Country.

Driving through San Antonio on a Friday afternoon (or any afternoon) is a real challenge to one's nerves and to one's marriage. Several times Champ said he thought we ought to turn around and head for home (or, better yet, to the deer lease). Traffic was horrific for about 30 miles north of downtown, but then thinned out as we neared Blanco. The rolling hills we used to know were now covered with new houses and new subdivisions. It didn't look the same as when we used to drive to the deer lease near Stonewall when the boys were small.

The last few miles were very picturesque-rolling hills, goats grazing along the highway's edge, lovely scenes of the Pedernales River flowing by-but not truly appreciated due to a car behind me, urging me to go faster than I really cared to go. Jimmie had come out to the highway to be sure we didn't pass by the ranch and it was a good thing. He tried to hail us down but I was going way too fast to stop. I managed to turn into a neighbor's drive not too far down the road, make the u-turn and head back.

Lots of Jimmie's and Bubba's old friends came to the party. Some we knew and some we had only heard about. We were particularly pleased to see our old friends from Donna, Bobby and Norma Green, and to meet some of those we had heard stories about over the years.

The food was marvelous and the band was excellent. They didn't miss a beat. Most of us were too old to really get out on the dance floor and enjoy the Cajun music, but we could still clap our hands in time to the rhythm. Champ and I did manage one or two dances, but they lasted way too many minutes. (Both of us were sore the next day.)

The second-floor guest room was wonderfully arranged. There were great views of the pond and the pasture from the big windows. During the early morning hours, a fierce electrical storm blew right through the area. The winds blew and the rain pounded against the windows while lightning flashed all around. It was terribly exciting and quite a change from the normal "northers" that come through the Valley.

As we headed back to Donna the next morning, we agreed it was well worth a little time and energy to spend an evening with old friends. It was even worth a 650-mile drive.

Corpus Christi - 2005

In early June, Champ and I drove off to visit the King Ranch Museum located in Sarita, Texas. He had heard how impressive and informative it was and wanted to see for himself. It took less than two hours to get there, but it took nearly that long to look around the facility and listen to the taped history of the South Texas area. It was fascinating to learn about the vaqueros. The skills they used nearly a hundred years ago have been incorporated into today's modern techniques of roping, riding and herding cattle. The King and Kenedy family histories are well known, and they made a profound impact on the economic development of the region during the early part of the 19th century.

We tried to visit the original King Ranch home site just outside of Kingsville, but we were too late for the last scheduled tour. Soooo we took off for our bed-and-breakfast stay at the Blutcher House in Corpus. We pulled up in front of the 100-year old home late in the afternoon and had difficulty getting inside the picket fence. We also had trouble getting in the front door but, fortunately for us, another guest had his key and let us in. It was a wonderful old home which had been restored by the Corpus Christi Junior Service League and it was situated on the bluff overlooking the bay. It was a step back in history.

The second-floor room we had offered a view of the gardens in the back of the house and a close-up look at the variety of trees there. I was enjoying the setting when a grey squirrel appeared from nowhere at my eye level and looked right back through the window at me. We stared at each other for a minute and then I think we both laughed. I know I did. Anyway, he scampered away and started chasing another squirrel of his own kind. It's not every day that you have an eye-to-eye encounter with a squirrel! How lucky I was to be there at the right time.

Another amusing occurrence was during my bubble bath. I was so pleased that bubbles were provided with the room, I didn't notice that the recently installed bathtub had the more-modern lower sides. It wasn't until I was in the tub with all the bubbles around me that I realized I was too big to lean back and relax in the relatively small amount of water the tub would hold. Soaking was out of the question! The bubbles barely covered my thighs. I sat there pondering the situation and then broke out into laughter. Laughing in the tub was a new experience for me. I had smiled on several occasions, but never laughed.

Our tour of the coastal area was not pre-planned and so we spent quite some time looking at new scenery. We headed north for about an hour and took a ferry ride over to Port Aransas. Then we took a side trip to Mustang Island and got caught in the traffic going to the sand sculpture show on the beaches of Padre Island. Somewhere along the way we took a wrong heading. Three hours after we left our B&B, we were right back where we started.

I think we laughed about that but I can't really remember. Oh, well, we wanted to see some different country and we did, twice!

Epilogue - Parting Words

My life has always been filled with laughter and I am thankful every day for that. I hope that I will still be laughing for another 20 or 30 years to come. With my family's history of longevity, it is possible. I expect tomorrow to be full of new opportunities for laughter, whether at home or on a world tour, and I look forward to those times with great anticipation.

I would like to share a few thoughts I have managed to formulate over the years and I address these words of advice mainly to the female audience, but I suppose they could be adapted quite nicely to the men out there as well.

When your spouse asks you to go somewhere, go. Don't think of all the reasons not to go; think how blessed you are that he wants to spend his favorite pastime with you by his side.

Make the best of it when you get where he's going and it isn't what you thought it might be. Don't grumble! It won't change anything.

Laugh as though you loved every minute of the time there. Tell your friends how much you enjoyed it; you might begin to believe it yourself.

Laughter is a wonderful gift from God. Be thankful for it and share it with others. A smile really is contagious! Let's all get infected!!!

About the Author

Camille Johnston Jones was raised in Mercedes, Texas, a small rural community in deep South Texas, during the 1940's and 1950's. She received her B.A. Degree from Southern Methodist University in Dallas in 1963 and moved with her husband, Forrest L.(Champ) Jones, to Donna, Texas, in 1965. After a short teaching career, she devoted her time and energies to raising their three sons, Michael, Matthew and Mitchell. She thoroughly enjoyed the small-town life and was very active in church and community activities. At the tender age of 43, she returned to the workforce and became the office manager in her husband's law firm.